# The Atonement

By
Edwin Reiner

**TEACH Services, Inc.**
Brushton, New York

Copyright © 2001 Edwin Reiner
ISBN 1-57258-191-3

*Published by*

**TEACH Services, Inc.**
254 Donovan Road
Brushton, New York 12916

"For if, when we were enemies, we were reconciled to God by the death of his Son, much more, being reconciled, we shall be saved by his life.

"And not only so, but we also joy in God through our Lord Jesus Christ, by whom we have now received the atonement."

Romans 5:10, 11.

# DEDICATED

to my wife, Rosalie

# CONTENTS

# Foreword

This book resulted from many years of doubts and misgivings, of searching and questioning, of rejecting and accepting. I had to know the truth as to how a person might find himself acceptable to God.

I was not always concerned with the science of salvation, the method God has used to bring Adam's descendants back to at-one-ment with Him. My home was only averagely religious despite a sincere and devout mother, and as a youngster I attended church sporadically. But with the years my interest grew. After I graduated from the University of Oregon with a degree in biology, I was influenced to enroll at the College of Medical Evangelists, now the Medical School of Loma Linda University. For the first time I found myself in a genuinely Christian atmosphere, under the influence of a dedicated faculty. Here I developed a sincere desire to know more about God and the Bible.

I had heretofore comprehended but little regarding the nature of man as compared with God and the relation of man to his Maker. The role of Christ had never been at all clear to me.

Just what was expected of me as a Christian? I wondered. Must I be just like Christ in all matters, for was it not true that He was our example? How could I lead a life that would be fully acceptable when judged before the holy law of God?

Pitifully confused, I realized that friends and acquaintances, respected members of various churches, were no closer to living as Christ lived than was I.

My soul cried out for the solutions. If a man lived long enough, might he develop enough goodness to merit sufficient favor with God to make him a candidate for heaven? Or did some mystical change occur in the grave to make the dead pure enough to enter heaven?

Neither theory seemed logical or probable, and several more years passed before my good fortune led me to Pastor W. L. Bird, a retired minister then approaching ninety years of age. He had taught religion on the university level and had studied the sanctuary service, both typical and antitypical. This remarkable man was also an authority on Christology, the study of the person of Christ. He questioned me about my general knowledge of the Bible, and especially stressed the atonement. My answers did not satisfy Pastor Bird. Under his quiet guidance I discovered that an atonement was possible for me and for everyone.

Others have willingly given of their time and talent that this book might be completed. Elder Harry W. Lowe, of the General Conference of Seventh-day Adventists, and Dr. W. G. C. Murdoch, dean of the Theology Department of Andrews University, critically read each chapter before its final approval. Without their kind counsel and advice I would have missed many of the wonders of the atonement.

Cecil Coffey and C. A. (Bill) Oliphant, as well as the entire Book Department of Southern Publishing Association, assisted immeasurably in the early formation of the book.

Gertrude Ayala assisted with early drafts of some of the chapters. Carolyn Crane and Charles Carson gave invaluable literary advice in formulating the final manuscript.

Delores Peterson, before her untimely death, inspired me to study deeply into the things of God and to come to a clearer understanding of the meaning of righteousness by faith.

Actually, the term "righteousness by faith" is the paramount subject of the book, but it will not be found once within its pages. I chose the word *atonement* because it reveals what righteousness by faith will accomplish—at-one-ment with God. Atonement is a seldom-used word; therefore its connotations are limited. To the majority, it means simply acceptance by God without definitely stating how the act is performed.

"Righteousness by faith," however, is a familiar phrase which Christians readily accept in lieu of the alternative, "righteousness by works." The difficulty in referring to "righteousness by faith" lies in the wide variety of notions of what it means, making it impossible to discuss it to advantage. Hence THE ATONEMENT. It contains the knowledge of how Heaven can declare an unrighteous being as righteous as though he had never sinned. Here is the clarification of "righteousness by faith," and here is a revelation of God's love as seen in the person of Jesus Christ.

The atonement is the key to eternal life in the world made new.

It is deeply satisfying to me to give you this message of hope and encouragement.

EDWIN W. REINER

# Preface

The plan of atonement connects the symbols and prophecies of the Old Testament with the life and teaching of Jesus Christ and the apostles, making the Bible a complete and harmonious whole. Conceived in the mind of God before creation, made known after the fall of man, symbolized in the patriarchal and Aaronic systems of worship, and consummated in the life of Christ on earth and in His ministry in the heavenly sanctuary, it reveals the sad results of sin, the suffering and sacrifice of the Deity, and the unfathomable depths of His love for the fallen human race.

This plan which arrests the progress of sin will terminate in the punishment and destruction of Satan and all who reject God's mercy, while those accepting it will be saved and live in the everlasting restoration of their Eden home.

Thus the atonement makes the plan of creation safe for all the universe throughout eternity and vindicates the holy character of its sovereign Author.

# 1

# Lucifer to Satan

BEFORE one studies the atonement, he needs to know the reason for it. Since the atonement is an answer to the problem of evil, a person should know how evil originated. The Bible contains no greater mystery than the fact that Lucifer was once the most exalted and majestic of God's created beings. He held the highest position in heaven, being next to Christ. God chose him to be the first covering cherub, a shining seraph on a throne of his own. The angelic hosts loved and respected him. In turn, Lucifer worshiped and adored his Creator.

To attempt to grasp how a noble, majestic being could become the devil, one must realize that God the Father and Christ had always known about the eventual apostasy of Satan, and the fall of Adam because of Lucifer's power of deception. They had designed the plan of salvation from eternity to counteract the working of evil in the universe.

Having been educated in the courts of heaven by God Himself, Lucifer was well acquainted with the Deity's character. Indeed, he had delighted in the high principles of heaven. But because of his beauty and his exalted position, he began to admire his own excellence and brilliance of mind. He thought of himself as being on an equality with Deity. Jealousy and envy gradually possessed him, so gradually that it was scarcely perceptible. He coveted Christ's superior position. Seeing no valid reason why he should not be included in the councils of heaven when the Godhead planned for the created intelligences, he did not realize that he was seeking a position that would have caused his own destruction, for he did not have power to create or to independently sustain his own existence.

Lucifer was well aware of the requirement, "Thou shalt have no other gods before me," but he began to dispute the justice of it. He believed it to be unnecessary. "I will ascend into heaven," he told himself. "I will exalt my throne above the stars of God: I will sit also upon the mount of the congregation, in the sides of the north: I will ascend above the heights of the clouds; I will be like the most High." Isaiah 14:13, 14.

The Old Testament prophet Ezekiel, in a vision about the king of Tyre, saw beyond the human ruler to the source of evil, Lucifer. "Thou sealest up the sum, full of wisdom, and perfect in beauty," Ezekiel commented about the fallen angel. "Thou hast been in Eden, the garden of God; every precious stone was thy covering, the sardius, topaz, and the diamond, the beryl, the onyx, and the jasper, the sapphire, the emerald, and the carbuncle, and gold. . . . Thou art the anointed cherub that covereth; and I have set thee so; thou wast upon the holy mountain of God; thou hast walked up and down in the midst of the stones of fire. Thou wast perfect in thy ways from the day that thou wast created, till iniquity was found in thee. . . .

"I will cast thee to the ground, I will lay thee before kings, that they may behold thee. . . . I will bring thee to ashes upon the earth in the sight of all them that behold thee. All they that know thee among the people shall be astonished at thee: thou shalt be a terror, and never shalt thou be any more." Ezekiel 28:12-19.

Only God dictates the duty of men and angels. They must

obey His law whether or not any authority enforces it or gives reward for obedience. Lucifer, the "son of the morning," unfitted himself for heaven by his voluntary rebellion. God did not dethrone him at once, however. He remained in heaven for a long period, being offered pardon again and again if he would repent and submit to the law of God.

His determined resistance finally so hardened his heart that repentance became impossible for him. He then openly accused the Creator of being a tyrant. God, he maintained, was selfish. He required self-denial of others, but He was not willing to deny Himself. "He will make slaves of us yet if we do not assert our liberty now," Lucifer shouted. "Follow me, and I will give you freedom!"

It has been said that genuine rebellion is incurable. Lucifer had become Satan, the enemy of God, the hater, the accuser. By the use of cunning, deceit, and lies, he masked his true purpose and presented himself before the angels as a great benefactor seeking their highest interest. He had a masterly, compelling influence over those who decided to give him their allegiance. But heaven could no longer tolerate him and the vast numbers who joined him in active rebellion against the government of God. A battle, as real as any fought on earth, waged in the Holy City. After a desperate struggle God evicted the evil angels from His courts. Their forced ejection made it necessary to take measures to prevent them from ever entering through the gates of heaven again.

"And there appeared another wonder in heaven; and behold a great red dragon, having seven heads and ten horns, and seven crowns upon his heads. And his tail drew the third part of the stars of heaven, and did cast them to the earth."

"And there was war in heaven: Michael and his angels fought against the dragon; and the dragon fought and his angels; and prevailed not; neither was their place found any more in heaven. And the great dragon was *cast out,* that old serpent, called the Devil, and Satan, which deceiveth the whole world: he was cast out into the earth, and his angels were cast out with him." Revelation 12:3, 4, 7-9.

When Satan fully realized that he was actually shut out of the beautiful City, remorse filled his heart. He implored the Creator to take him back, to allow him to fill any position at all which God cared to assign him.

But Satan felt no genuine repentance. His character was too hopelessly ruined. He sorrowed only for what he had lost. Satan desired knowledge which God had never designed that he should have, and his persistent efforts to pry into the secrets of Deity had brought their just reward.

When Satan became convinced that the decision was irrevocable, his anguish turned to rage. He planned to marshal his sympathizers into an army and resume his warfare against Deity. Especially would he attack the new being God had just created. He would wrest the earth from him. He would then set up his own headquarters and throne on this planet in opposition to that of the Creator. The descendants of Adam would provide him additional forces to join in an unholy alliance with the hosts of evil.

After Adam's fall, Satan claimed that the human race must also be forever shut from God's favor, because God had banished him, man's ruler, from heaven. Were they not just as deserving as he of punishment? he reasoned. He declared that forgiveness was impossible for Adam unless God also forgave him and the rebellious angels. To do otherwise would be grossly unfair.

To his surprise he learned that God was providing a plan of atonement for man. Grace was a new manifestation of God's

16

character, a mystery beyond Satan's comprehension.

Even though he could not enter again into the heavenly courts, Satan continued to annoy and harass the unfallen angels at every opportunity. He stationed himself at heaven's gates, becoming an "accuser of . . . [the] brethren," flaunting the sins of Christ's professed followers before the loyal angels. There he boasted he could bring God's faithful servant Job under his dominion, and there he stood whenever "the sons of God" came to present themselves before the Lord, that he might introduce his insidious theories and make his insulting assertions.

For four thousand years Satan exercised his power of deception to cause man to sink ever lower in moral degradation.

Having captured the mind of man, the great deceiver held the earth largely under his control. All men had bowed in obeisance to his rule and had broken the law of God. All deserved destruction. When the Son of God came to earth to free men from the tyranny of Satan, the image of God had nearly vanished in those who had once been the noblest of His creation next to the angels. To the watching universe, mankind appeared almost worthless. That Christ should stoop to reclaim such apparently useless material caused wonder and amazement among the angels.

When the Redeemer came to the earth, Satan unceasingly directed his attacks against Him. He watched every movement of Christ's life and endeavored to entice Him with a multitude of temptations. He who had once been exalted in the courts of heaven still aimed to be the highest power in the universe. If he could conquer the Son of God in His humanity, then he felt confident he could eventually conquer all of God's creation.

But the inhabitants of heaven and the unfallen worlds observed Satan's cruelty and cunning, and every blow Satan inflicted upon Christ rebounded upon himself. By his treatment of Christ, Satan clearly demonstrated the falseness of his own attributes and of his pretensions as the friend of God. Upon Christ's death on the cross, Satan fell forever from the sympathy of the heavenly angels. "And I heard a loud voice saying in heaven, Now is come salvation, and strength, and the kingdom of our God, and the power of his Christ: for the accuser of our brethren is *cast down,* which accused them before God day and night." Revelation 12:10.

The unfallen beings had loved Lucifer as their leader in the courts of God. Even after his expulsion from heaven, some shreds of sympathy for him remained in the minds of the inhabitants of various planets. But after Christ's death on the cross it instantly vanished. Now that he had fully unmasked his character by bringing Jesus to the cross, the last link between himself and the loyal angels broke. Christ's death forever silenced Satan's charges that God would not deny Himself.

But so cruel and powerful a foe could not give up the battle. As long as time lasts, he will do all in his power to prevent fallen man from accepting the justification before God provided by the cross. He has an intense and personal interest in every individual, for he knows that he must suffer the final punishment for every sin he has caused the redeemed to commit. He tells himself that it may still be possible for him to gain the ultimate advantage.

Since Adam's fall, Satan has opposed God's effort to redeem the human race. He tempts men, step by step, away from God, then turns to accuse them of the sins he caused them to commit. They become discouraged and lose confidence in themselves and in Christ's pardoning love. Satan claims them as his own followers. He points to their lives and says, "They profess to be Thy children, but they are my property!" He demands to be allowed to destroy them, but Jesus restrains him.

As God's people approach the perils of the days before Christ's second coming, Satan will work with feverish cunning. Disguised as an angel of light, he will lead many to accept false doctrines that will sap the foundations of their faith. The Bible warns that the "very elect" are in danger of being deceived. (Matthew 24:24; Mark 13:22.)

When the last spiritual battle has been fought and the victory won, Satan must receive his final reward. The universe will then see how inexcusable sin is, and that its existence cannot be justified. Those who chose to join him in rebellion must share in his reward. "The day that cometh shall burn them up, saith the Lord of hosts." Malachi 4:1. "And the devil that deceived them was *cast into* the lake of fire and brimstone, where the beast and the false prophet are, and shall be tormented day and night for ever and ever." Revelation 20:10.

The following chapters portray the method God used to redeem man—how He has revealed it to the human race, how it works, and how it makes eternal life available to man. Understanding the atonement is one of the most vital tasks facing the Christian.

# 2

# Mediatorial Worship

CHRISTIANS generally refer to Christ's death on the cross as the atonement, but the doctrine of the atonement involves much more than His death. It also includes His life of perfect obedience to God's law. But even more, atonement comprises a series of related occurrences extending throughout eternity. It is a process rather than a single event.

Man must realize that he has nothing to do with reconciling himself with God. He has only the privilege of accepting or rejecting the reconciliation provided by God.

God pronounced the death sentence upon Adam and his descendants when he disobeyed God's specific request not to eat any of the fruit from the tree of the knowledge of good and evil. To eat the fruit revealed a distrust of God and His truthfulness. The punishment offered no escape. Because the law demanded the life of the guilty, man found himself in a hopeless situation. He could not himself approach God in order to make an atonement for his sin. A criminal cannot forgive himself if he has broken a law. Only those who framed the law or administer it can do that. Consequently, no created being—man or angel—could forgive man. Only a member of the Godhead could free him from the results of sin.

Adam and the entire race were lost unless God would help. Job recognized his position when he cried out desperately, "Neither is there any daysman betwixt us, that might lay his hand upon us both." Job 9:33. "Daysman" is a word somewhat equivalent to the modern term "umpire" or "arbiter."

The entrance of sin through Lucifer had confronted God and all creation with a problem of great magnitude. Someone had challenged the law of the universe. Was God a tyrant? Was He unjust? Was He waiting to destroy the disobedient? All beings waited God's reaction to the crisis.

The rebellion of Adam supplied Satan with a convincing argument and example to present before the other worlds that had never sinned. Satan asserted that created beings could not possibly obey God's law and that it was inherently unjust. Therefore, through mankind God must demonstrate the justice of His law, and at the same time show mercy to the sinner.

Before the creation of the earth God had conceived His plan to justify Himself and His law. Like the law, "it was ordained by angels in the hand of a mediator." (Galatians 3:19.)

God gave Adam and Eve a period of probation in which to return to their allegiance to Him. Their posterity would also share this plan of benevolence. After Adam's fall, Christ became his instructor. He took upon Himself the role of Mediator between God and man, thus saving the human race from immediate death. In time, He would reveal Himself in human form, holding a position at the head of humanity and taking the nature but not the sinfulness of man.

God promised Isaiah, "The Redeemer shall come to Zion, and unto them that turn from transgression in Jacob, saith the Lord." Isaiah 59:20.

God and Christ had made a covenant between themselves that would secure humanity's salvation, that would free mankind from its death sentence and offer it another opportunity for eternal existence. Christ had promised to take the punishment of the transgressor should man sin. In addition, He

21

would furnish the perfect life required of all inhabitants of the universe. By becoming man's substitute for sin and righteousness, Christ would satisfy all the claims of the law. He would provide every necessity for man's salvation.

But to be mankind's Saviour, Christ could not remain as God in heaven. So He offered to meet God's wrath in place of sinful man. He would take the responsibility for man's sins, and as a result of them He would suffer and die in the same manner as a sinner. Christ must first live a sin-free and perfect human life among men. Then He would be able to substitute His own perfect human life for that of any of His followers when they had to stand before God's judgment seat.

The Father and the Son had made their plans before mankind sinned, and even before the creation of the earth. To fulfill the plans, Christ had to come to the earth as a man. He had to assume human characteristics and temporarily suspend the use of His divine powers and attributes in His own behalf. Such a step man finds difficult to understand. He who coexisted with God and created the earth and the heavenly bodies condescended to come to earth as a man. He would take the nature of man, but not the sin. The Book of Hebrews, telling of Christ as Mediator between God and man, has much to say about the Saviour's humanity.

"But we see Jesus, who was made a little lower than the angels for the suffering of death, crowned with glory and honour; that he by the grace of God should taste death for every man."

"Forasmuch then as the children are partakers of flesh and blood, he also himself likewise took part of the same; that through death he might destroy him that had the power of death, that is, the devil."

"For verily he took not on him the nature of angels; but

he took on him the seed of Abraham." Hebrews 2:9, 14, 16.

Yet, throughout His stay on earth, Christ remained God in the highest sense. His humanity veiled His divinity in order that He might dwell among men without His power destroying them. "He hath no form nor comeliness; and when we shall see him, there is no beauty that we should desire him." Isaiah 53:2.

During His life on earth Christ was a singular combination of sinless humanity and Deity. Only through such a union could He serve as Mediator between God and mankind. Christ indeed represented the "daysman," or divine umpire, Job desired. Only a Being equal to God, possessing the attributes that would make Him worthy to intercede with the Infinite God in man's behalf, one who would also represent God to a fallen world, could reconcile God and man.

Man's substitute had to possess a man's nature, a connection with the human family whom He was to represent; and as God's ambassador, He had to share the divine nature. He could then bridge the gulf separating God and man. Christ became the only means of communication between the two after Adam and Eve sinned in the Garden of Eden. When He became incarnate, His role of Mediator took on wider significance, and He entered more actively into His mission of reconciliation. The office of Christ is to introduce God to man, and man to God.

Mediatorial worship, the worship of God through an intercessor, is peculiar to Christianity. Other religions teach the believer to come directly to his God for the forgiveness of sin. Under such provisions, the individual must atone for his own transgression, since he has no mediator to intercede for him. But the Bible teaches that sin severed all connections man had with God the Father, cutting the earth off from heaven. Christ

23

alone has spanned the gulf and made possible a route of communication. Non-Christian religions teach their adherents that they can personally do something to merit favor before their god, making them acceptable to their particular deity. The Christian, however, realizes his total dependence upon Christ in all things necessary for salvation. Man cannot directly approach God the Father except through Jesus Christ.

The principle of man being able to save himself through his own efforts lies at the foundation of every non-Christian religion. But through mediatorial worship the Christian recognizes his inferior status before God. The believer comes to understand that he is under the condemnation of God's law, subject to the death penalty, and that he must rely totally on the intercession of Christ.

Jesus Christ, as mankind's Mediator, has a vital work to do for the Christian believer. First, He sustains all life. His intervention allowed Adam to continue to live when he first rebelled. Christ came forward to take the penalty in man's stead. Such a step did not set justice aside. Rather it delayed the punishment until a later time. Had not Christ done so, mankind would not be alive today.

Christ as Mediator stood between God the Father and the human race. As Mediator He provides a way whereby the guilty sinner can find access to God. The sinner cannot come in his own person, with his guilt upon him, and with no greater merit than he possessed within himself. Only Christ can open the way.

As man's Saviour, Christ had to satisfy the law's stipulations—standards impossible for man to meet unaided. The sinner cannot escape the claims of the law upon his life, for he has broken it and he is guilty. For the transgressor to be acceptable before God, someone must pardon him and declare him sinless. Only one equal with the law can do so. The law is an expression of God's nature, and Christ is part of the Godhead. He who gave the law possesses the power to forgive sins. (See Genesis 49:10 and Matthew 9:6.) The authority that establishes a law also has the right and power to forgive its infraction.

The book *Life of Christ*, by Ellen G. White, in the section *Redemption: or the Temptation of Christ*, states that "Christ's work was to reconcile man to God through His human nature, and God to man through His divine nature." "In Christ were united the human and the divine. His mission was to reconcile God to man, and man to God. His work was to unite the finite with the Infinite."—Pp. 37, 33.

The Mediator must also save man from consciously committing sin—voluntarily increasing his alienation from God. "Now unto him that is able to keep you from falling, and to present you faultless before the presence of his glory with exceeding joy." Jude 24.

Christ changes the sinner. By beholding Christ's life, a man begins to assume his Saviour's characteristics and traits. He grows into the likeness of God. But he cannot transform himself through his own efforts. He needs Christ's strength and guidance.

The Mediator must make the believer acceptable to God and heaven, or the human being will face eternal death. Heaven will not tolerate any sinfulness. Only humanity as perfect as Adam was before he sinned can live with God.

Christ vicariously endured the penalty for the Christian's sin. He accepted the short span of death in Joseph's tomb so that the Christian could escape eternal death. And Christ's perfect relationship with God substitutes for the sinner's broken one. The believer shares Christ's character. After Christ's second coming, even the angels in heaven will stand in awe of the redeemed, who through the atonement have reached the position God originally intended for them.

Man must understand that God did not arbitrarily refuse to deal directly with him after Adam sinned. It was actually impossible for God to do so. God's nature and power would instantly have destroyed fallen man. Only after man is changed and glorified at Christ's second coming will he be able to exist in the presence of God. The Apostle Paul says the change in man's nature will occur "in a moment, in the twinkling of an eye" as Christ returns to the earth. Prior to that time, man's only righteousness rests in his faith in the merits of his Mediator. But then the Christian will reflect the image of God and heaven, and he will become the citizen of a land "whose builder and maker is God." (Hebrews 11:10.)

The Mediator must also reveal God's nature to fallen humanity. The character of God has been misrepresented to mankind, and many have clothed the Father in the attributes of Satan. Satan has portrayed God as a supreme and all-powerful Being eagerly awaiting every opportunity to punish mankind. He has led men to term every terrible act and calamity as "the will of God." By the time of Christ's first advent, mankind had lost sight of the concept of God as a loving Father. It took Christ, who said, "I and my Father are one" (John 10: 30), to demonstrate God's infinite capacity to love humanity.

To have a Mediator in the courts of heaven is not merely to have a lawyer. An attorney in man's legal system represents the accused. He seeks to interpret the law in a favorable manner for his client. Should the court find the defendant guilty, the counsel for the defense will often attempt, by a series of legal maneuvers, to reduce the sentence. But Christ does much more. He actually has taken his client's penalty, accepted his sins, and died in his place.

Furthermore, He is willing to present man with the attributes of a holy and righteous life that he may be declared "Not guilty."

No attorney in the world would do such a thing. Neither would it be possible. Lawyers do not pay their clients' fines, nor do they go to prison for them—much less accept the death penalty.

# 3

# The Purpose of Creation

GOD'S creative power is as incomprehensible to the human mind as is His existence. Human science cannot explain how God created the world and its complex living organisms. Although man may not inquire into the process of creation, surely it is his privilege to study into the reason for his existence. Just what does God want to do with the earth? More specifically, what purpose does He have in mind for each individual?

Since God is omniscient, and thus knows the future, He knew long before the creation of the first angel that sin would enter the universe. His knowledge did not, however, deter Him from carrying out His plan for bringing into existence vast galaxies of inhabited worlds—planetary systems flawless in every detail.

It would not be easy to imagine a time before God created anything, but surely such a time did exist. In the vast aeons of the past there was a moment when the universe began. The first created angel, the first created world, came into existence.

Inasmuch as God knew sin would come, a question immediately arises regarding those who chose to disobey. Could God not have refrained from creating *them?* Could He not have substituted another seraph for Lucifer? or another man and woman in place of Adam and Eve? But since God endowed all beings as free moral agents, the results would have been the same. Some probably would have chosen to exercise their prerogative of free will unwisely. The development of sin cannot be explained, but God can in no way be blamed for its existence.

Only one way existed to avoid the development of evil in the universe. God could have chosen to have no creation at all, or He could have fashioned worlds populated by beings such as animals or automatons without the power of moral choice.

The plan for man's redemption was not an afterthought. Nor did God formulate it after the fall of Adam. Instead, it is a "revelation of the mystery, which was kept secret since the world began." Redemption unfolds principles that have always been the foundation of God's throne. From the beginning God the Father and Christ knew of the apostasy of Satan, and of the fall of man through the apostate's power.

It is important to know that God did not ordain that sin should exist. But He did foresee its existence and made provision to meet the terrible emergency.

Creation was a manifestation of God's love, and for age upon age, a universe of happy, harmonious intelligences basked in the glory of His love. Seraphim and cherubim and all the sons of God enjoyed the bounties of His creation, delighting to obey His every wish. But the love God expressed through His creative power did not prevent sin. All living beings, however, will witness and appreciate the love God demonstrated in His redemption of man. The universe will have observed the results of sin and will never fall prey to it again. Sin will be eradicated forever, and God's purpose in creation will reach its ultimate fulfillment.

After Satan's expulsion from heaven, the Father and the Son fulfilled their plan to create man. A great vacancy existed in the heavenly courts. Fully a third of the angels had been thrust out because of their loyalty to the deceiver. Those who had been their companions and who had worshiped with them around the throne of God felt their absence. God planned to fill the vacancies with the new beings He was about to call into existence.

God, in counsel with Christ, had formed the plan of creating man in His own image. At first man would live in a state of probation. He would face tests to prove his loyalty to God. Should he bear the first trial, he would not be tormented with continual temptations, but would be exalted, raised equal with the angels. The plan has not failed. Adam's fall only temporarily interrupted it. God had foreseen evil and had prepared to meet and overcome it. He would arrange events to place the universe on an eternal basis of security. Satan was given time to develop his concepts and ideas, for he claimed that they were superior to the principles of God. The entire universe must witness the results of Satan's rebellion in order that the government of God may stand vindicated.

In unison the Father and Son created man. By a word, matter appeared where there had been nothing. Life sprang into being, the energies of nature were organized to provide man with a glorious habitation. All the intelligences of the universe broke into rapturous song at the completion of the new world. Man was an exalted being.

Man had stood uppermost in the mind of God even before He brought the first angel into being, or formed the first world. The human race held a special place in God's thoughts, for His creation was for a special purpose. The earth would be the great stage on which would be dramatized the power of God's love. Here the contest between good and evil would come to a mighty climax before the eyes of all created intelligences. "For we are made a spectacle unto the world, and to angels, and to men," the Bible declares. (1 Corinthians 4:9.)

"And to make all men see what is the fellowship of the

mystery, which from the beginning of the world hath been hid in God, who created all things by Jesus Christ: *to the intent that now unto the principalities and powers in heavenly places might be known by the church the manifold wisdom of God, according to the eternal purpose which he purposed in Christ Jesus our Lord,"* Ephesians 3:9-11 states as the purpose of human creation. It is important to consider that it was not merely to accomplish the redemption of man that Christ came to earth. *He wanted to demonstrate to all the worlds that God's law is unchangeable, and that the result of sin is death.*

The struggle between the forces of sin and those of righteousness would take place in the mind and heart of every son and daughter of Adam, with the earth itself as the final battlefield between Satan and Christ.

Each man, woman, and child plays an equally important part in fulfilling God's purpose for the universe. Whether man accepts or rejects the plan of atonement, his life testifies to the wisdom of God's principles for His creatures. If he refuses the offered salvation, he shows how the disobedient destroy themselves. If he accepts God's gift, he demonstrates that obedience to the Deity means eternal life. But probably the most important point to keep in mind is that *God brought mankind into existence because He needed him.*

It must prove a baffling mystery to Satan that God could choose to repopulate heaven with such beings. He knows how far he has caused them to reject God and His principles, and how little resemblance they bear to the seraphim and cherubim in the heavenly courts. His selfish mind cannot comprehend the plan of redemption. That Christ should step down from His throne and humiliate Himself more and more in the sight of heaven fills Satan with amazement. To him the redeemed throng seem just as deserving of punishment as is he himself.

31

Satan criticizes man in the presence of God, declaring that man has by his sins forfeited divine protection. He claims the right to destroy them as transgressors. He pronounces them just as deserving of exclusion from God's favor as he is. "Are these the people who are to take my place in heaven," he asks, "and the place of the angels who united with me?"

But Jesus will silence him. Christ came to earth to dispute the authority of Satan, who claims supremacy over it. He came to restore in mankind the defaced image of God, to elevate and refine and make humanity fit for companionship with the angels—if each individual will let Him have His way in his life. And when the great contest ends, mankind will take the position in the courts of God which Satan and his angels lost through their rebellion.

The plan of redemption and the plan of creation went hand in hand. The one was necessary to ensure the ultimate perfection of the other. Nothing can frustrate God's purpose in creation. For mankind to know that they exist here because God needs them gives new dimension to one's understanding of the plan of salvation. We see that man is exceedingly valuable to God, and we come to regard one's duty to fellow members of the human family with a sacred awe. We see humanity as precious in God's sight, and we know that nothing can turn aside His immense love and care for those for whom He made such a costly sacrifice.

# 4

# The Three Dispensations

SCRIPTURE divides the world's history into three distinct religious periods. Biblical scholars have termed them *dispensations*. In its broadest sense, the word *dispensation* gives clarity to one's study of the atonement. One Bible dictionary defines a dispensation as "the charge of proclaiming the Gospel of Christ (1 Corinthians 9:17; Ephesians 3:2). Also the scheme, or plan of God's dealings with men. In the Patriarchal, Mosaic, and Christian periods God has commented—enlarged and perfected His revelation of Himself in His Grace to this world (Ephesians 1:10; Colossians 1:25). The whole development of His great plan has been gradual, and adapted at every stage to the existing state of the human family."

The Son of God stands at the center of the great plan of redemption. "Neither is there salvation in any other: for there is none other name under heaven given among men, whereby we must be saved." Acts 4:12.

God's covenant of grace is the same through all periods of time. In every age God saves man in exactly the same manner. Only the method of worshiping through a mediator has varied. These divinely appointed methods have differed to meet the peculiar needs of mankind in each of the three dispensations. God has made known to man the doctrine of reconciliation to an ever-increasing extent over the ages, and the world has received greater revelations of God's love with each passing generation.

At times, man has cherished such knowledge. Great blessings then resulted from acting upon it. At other times, he has despised it, producing a period of spiritual darkness and misery. But in every age faithful and devout followers of Christ have courageously believed and advocated the knowledge they had. Of them, the Scriptures tell us, "the world was not worthy," for they were hated, persecuted, hunted, and tortured. Many believers died because of their faith.

The Book of Genesis covers the longest of the three divisions of time—a period called the patriarchal dispensation. This first book of Moses records 2,500 years of history, beginning with the creation of the world and extending to the birth of the nation of Israel at the foot of Mount Sinai. For most of the period, especially the centuries before the Noachian Flood, no written revelations of God's will existed. Those men of giant intellect had no need for the printed word. Knowledge passed from father to son, each generation instructing the next with clear and unimpaired memory. Angels often visited with men, and Christ Himself spoke face to face with some of the patriarchs.

People worshiped differently then. With no Scriptures, no hymnals, no church buildings or sanctuaries, they assembled for religious services according to God's direction. Each family unit composed a church entity. The patriarch, the father of the family, presided over the group. Many of the family units were larger in number than present-day churches. Abraham's household, for example, comprised nearly a thousand members.

In those days the birthright came down through the eldest son, who became the patriarch upon the death of his father. Great responsibility rested upon the patriarch, for he was also the priest of his family.

God Himself ordained a sacrificial system in which the

patriarch ministered for his family. As mediator, the patriarchal priest assumed the guilt of the repentant sinner. In this he typified Christ. Through his mediation the sinner looked across the gulf of ages to the Lamb of God that takes away the sin of the world.

The morning and evening altar ceremony, with the priest and the sacrificial lamb, served as God's method for teaching man the plan of salvation. The stranger and the wayfarer who stopped to watch the sacred outdoor worship service heard lessons from the lips of the patriarchal priests which they did not soon forget. The covenant given to Adam and Noah, and again to Abraham and Melchizedek, and the symbolic ladder shown Jacob in a dream, all pointed forward to the role of Jesus as Mediator. The sale of Joseph into Egypt and his later act of saving his family aptly illustrate the work of the Saviour of mankind. The Book of Job shows that believers in patriarchal days had an insight into the mysteries of redemption.

This first and longest of the dispensations appropriately ended at the foot of Mount Sinai. In fulfillment of the promise made to Abraham, Israel became a nation under God, with a theocratic form of government. The family altar service with its daily atonement gave way to the Levitical priesthood and the ceremonial law of the sanctuary. The second period carries various titles such as the Jewish, Levitical, or legal dispensation.

God chose the descendants of Aaron to act as priests for the entire nation. For 1,500 years the Hebrew nation represented the depository of God's law in the world, and believers worshiped Him in a manner far different from the age which had passed away.

About this time, men, under the Holy Spirit's direction, began to write the Scriptures, for nothing pertaining to the great principles of atonement could now be trusted to man's failing memory. Adam's descendants had lessened both in stature and wisdom, but God would not leave man with the excuse that he lacked a knowledge of the divine will. At Sinai He recorded His sacred law on the most durable material to be had—stone—using His own finger to write it. At the same time He proclaimed His covenant audibly in the hearing of the entire Jewish populace. The sanctuary service pointed out that God had not given the law to make men righteous, but to show them their great spiritual need. The Levitical priesthood and ceremonial law demonstrated the plan of salvation as nothing else could. Through such means God kept alive faith in the coming of the Messiah.

Israel continued the patriarchal practice of confessing sins and offering praise to the great Lawgiver each morning and evening, even as many consecrated Christians do today. In the wilderness the Hebrews gathered around the sanctuary at the sacred hours of worship while the priest slew the sacrificial lamb. Through the offering of incense believers not only learned of Christ's sacrificial death, but also of His perfect life of obedience, which would be offered to God in place of their own failures and imperfections. As His role as Mediator became more clear and distinct, the people came to realize that their actual lives depended upon the work of the priest.

Sometimes Bible scholars refer to the patriarchal and Levitical dispensations as one, calling it "the old dispensation." Some Christians feel that the period was a time of spiritual and intellectual darkness, and that the Old Testament has no value now as a spiritual guide. The New Testament has taken its place, they believe.

Nothing could be less true. The New Testament does not contain a new religion or gospel. Rather, it unfolds the Old, for the prophets of God spoke less for their own time than they did for the future. Paul says, "All these things happened unto them for ensamples: and they are written for our admonition, upon whom the ends of the world are come." 1 Corinthians 10:11. The apostles unite their witness to the teachings of the prophets, and together they present a complete outline of the plan of salvation.

As time passes and prophecy fulfills, men gain greater understanding of salvation. But such additional knowledge does not entitle anyone to scorn or ridicule the historical development of theology. The life and death of Christ give significance to the whole Jewish religious system. He integrates the old and new dispensations.

Theologians have occasionally called the gospel era the dispensation of the Holy Spirit. More frequently they refer to it as the new dispensation. Christ's statement when dying on the cross, "It is finished," ushered it in. At the same moment unseen hands rent the veil of the earthly sanctuary from top to bottom, signifying that type had now met antitype, actuality had replaced symbol. Men would approach God "by a new and living way." (Hebrews 10:20.)

The ceremonial law, a system of regulations and rituals designed specifically for the Jews, ceased forever. Christ's chosen people had divorced themselves from Him and irrevocably terminated the theocracy. A new people would take the place of literal Israel, and the Godhead would count all who accepted Christ as belonging to spiritual Israel. Christ ascended to the right hand of His Father to plead for all who would transfer their sins to Him by faith.

The new spiritual era brought to light all the blessings of the Abrahamic covenant. Under the guidance of the Holy Spirit men now approach God through their human-divine Priest. For two thousand years the Holy Spirit has ministered in the midst of the church on earth, a spiritual nation composed of true believers throughout the world.

The Comforter—as Christ termed the Holy Spirit—has been pointing the minds of men to the divine High Priest, who has gone "to prepare a place" (John 14:2, 3) in the courts of God for all who accept His mediation. The Holy Spirit teaches men about the process of atonement now going on in the sanctuary in heaven, and He causes them to feel the need of reconciliation. He gives men repentance and brings confession from their lips. When men do not resist and reject the Holy Spirit's influence, He leads them by the compelling power of God's love to accept the results of Christ's life on earth and His sacrifice on the cross.

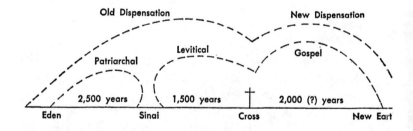

# 5

# Reconciliation in the First Apartment

AS POINTED OUT earlier, as important as the death of Christ on the cross was, it could not and did not finish the work of atonement which God and Christ ordained before the earth ever existed. His sacrificial death at Golgotha completed one phase of His work of reconciliation. Because of Adam's transgression, the human race had no channel of communication between man and God other than through Jesus Christ. Only His life of perfection and His death could raise humanity in moral value with God. Humanity then had a member who had gained the right to enter into the presence of God, one who was sinless and would not be consumed by God's glory. Mankind now had Someone to finish the work of atonement.

Although Christ had completed His preparatory task of reconciling humanity as a whole to God in the court of the heavenly sanctuary—the earth—He now had a role in the apartments of the heavenly sanctuary which would finalize the atonement. Through this work He would fully reconcile God to man.

In the typical service, the sprinkling of the blood of the sin offering by the priest in the court or his act of eating some of the sacrifice, both of which symbolically passed the sins of the Jewish nation on to him, only half completed the atonement. "Wherefore have ye not eaten the sin offering in the holy place, seeing it is most holy, and God hath given it you to bear the iniquity of the congregation, to make atonement

39

for them before the Lord?" Leviticus 10:17. The sin bearer must take the sins into the holy places for the religious ceremony to be effective. The priests had to meet the demands and requirements of God's law through the symbolic offerings of blood and incense.

Similarly, the actual atonement conducted in the true tabernacle—which the one Moses had built symbolized—began in the earth, the court of the heavenly sanctuary. As the human priest still had an important work to perform in the holy places, so Christ had much to do in the tabernacle "not made with hands." Christ's death reconciled mankind to God, but only His perfect life will satisfy God the Father's sense of justice and save humanity from the penalty of eternal death.

"And all things are of God, who hath reconciled us to himself by Jesus Christ, and hath given to us the ministry of reconciliation; to wit, that God was in Christ, reconciling the world unto himself, not imputing their trespasses unto them; and hath committed unto us the word of reconciliation.

"Now then we are ambassadors for Christ, as though God did beseech you by us: we pray you in Christ's stead, be ye reconciled to God.

"For he hath made him to be sin for us, who knew no sin; that we might be made the righteousness of God in him." 2 Corinthians 5:18-21.

The sacrifice of the red heifer presented an impressive spectacle deep with spiritual meaning. God instituted the service to purify those ceremonially defiled from contact with the dead. The animal offered was red, the color of blood. As with all Hebrew sacrifices, it pointed to the death of Christ. Furthermore, the animal could not have any physical imperfections, nor could it have ever worn a yoke, for it represented Christ, who voluntarily came to accomplish the atonement.

No power—either in heaven or earth—coerced Christ into making His decision to save man. He was independent and above all law.

Attendants led the sacrificial heifer outside the camp and slew the animal in a most imposing manner. The ritual symbolized Christ's suffering outside the gates of Jerusalem, indicating that the Saviour died for all mankind, not for the Hebrews alone. After the death of the animal, a service involving the sin free blood of the heifer, the ashes of the completely burned victim, and water from a running stream purified those considered ceremonially unclean.

The thoroughness of the ritual symbolized the completeness of the work of Christ in cleansing the repentant sinner. The Hebrew priest took the sacrificial blood into the sanctuary as a propitiation for sin. Today, in the gospel dispensation, Christ as High Priest ministers in the tabernacle in heaven, where He is reconciling God to man. After having shed His blood on the cross, He entered into the holy place—the first compartment.

In the typical service, the Tabernacle became defiled all year by the record of Israel's confessed sins. In order to reconcile God to man completely, these sins had to be atoned for—eradicated—because the record stood between God and man.

God loves the sinner, but He hates the sin. For God to be reconciled to man He must not only pardon the sins of those who would repent, but also declare them to be, as the Bible puts it, "as white as snow." They must stand before God's law as though they had never sinned. Such was the ministry God commanded the human priest to perform in the Jewish Tabernacle. And such is the ministry of Christ, our true Priest, in the better sanctuary in heaven.

The mystery of redemption lies in the fact that God the Fa-

41

ther permitted His innocent, pure, and holy Son to bear the punishment deserved by a thankless race of rebels against the divine government that, through the manifestation of His love, they might stand before Him repentant, as guiltless as though they had never sinned. Angels in heaven marveled that God should rest His wrath on the Son, that Christ should exchange a life of infinite value in the heavenly courts for the worthless existence of a race of beings degraded by sin.

The fourth chapter of Leviticus vividly describes the spectacular sin offering service which taught the Hebrews deep, profound truths. This service symbolized the transfer of sin to the Tabernacle and provisionally freed the sinner of his guilt. His sins now symbolically rested on the priest and on the sacrificial lamb, and their record waited in the sanctuary for the Day of Atonement.

Similar events transpired when Christ died as the one great sacrifice for sin. Because of His death in the court of the heavenly sanctuary—the earth—all the confessed sins of spiritual Israel could be transferred to the sanctuary "not made with hands." When the "Lamb of God, which taketh away the sin of the world," gave up His life on the cross, His death created a medium by which the sins of the repentant could be transferred into the "Holiest of all." That medium is the blood of Christ.

"Having therefore, brethren, boldness to enter into the holiest by the blood of Jesus, by a new and living way, which he hath consecrated for us, through the veil, that is to say, his flesh." Hebrews 10:19, 20. The shed blood stands for the act Christ performed to end the alienation between God and man.

The phrase "into the holiest" obviously has reference to the sanctuary in heaven, for the apostle is comparing the earthly Tabernacle with the celestial one. The second apartment is not implied here. Rather, the thought expressed is a continuation of that found in Hebrews 9:8: "The Holy Ghost this signifying, that the way into the holiest of all was not yet made manifest, while as the first tabernacle was yet standing." The author of Hebrews is simply saying that the heavenly sanctuary is more holy than the Hebrew one.

Further evidence that Christ went directly into the first apartment is found by studying the Jewish Tabernacle ceremony. In it the priest carried the blood of the sin offering directly into the first apartment. Never did the blood go into the second apartment during the yearly ministration. Only the blood of the priest's bullock and the Lord's goat, upon which no sin was confessed, passed into the most holy place, the second apartment. This event occurred but once a year, on the Day of Atonement.

The reference to "a new and living way," of course, indicates the means of approaching God through the new Priest of Israel, Christ, the one Mediator between man and God. No longer would slain animals be symbolic vehicles to approach God. Now, through the ministry of the heavenly sanctuary and the divine sacrifice of Christ, the sinner has atonement with God.

When Christ died on the cross of Calvary, a new channel of communication with God opened to both Jew and Gentile. The Saviour would from then on officiate as Priest and Advocate before God the Father. Animal sacrifices no longer had any value. Men no longer needed to worship God through a human mediator. Type had met antitype.

At His baptism in the River Jordan Christ assumed responsibility for the sins of every man—past, present, future. (See chapter 19.) There the "Lamb of God" began the trek that would lead Him to the cross. Here in the court—the planet earth—He shed the blood He would offer with the incense, or merit, of His righteous life in the antitypical holy places. The Holy Spirit descended upon Jesus when He came to be baptized by John. At His baptism He received anointing for His work as man's high priest. Here John proclaimed Him to be "the Lamb of God, which taketh away the sin of the world." It would be three years, the age of the lamb of the Levitical daily service, before this holy Lamb would come to the altar of Calvary.

After His resurrection He was anointed again, this time at the throne of God, surrounded by all the heavenly beings. At that time He began another phase of His work as man's High Priest. The event occurred at Pentecost, ten days after His ascension, and fifty days after He arose from the grave. His resurrection occurred on the day the Jewish priests offered the wave sheaf, which symbolized Christ and those resurrected with Him, the firstfruits of those who sleep. As their Saviour was being anointed in heaven, the Holy Spirit descended to the waiting disciples.

From eternity the heavenly sanctuary had been God's dwelling place. It was the center of His kingdom. With the entrance of sin, the Godhead had made provisions for the atonement. Now heaven prepared the celestial tabernacle for the entrance of the Priest. Soon Christ would begin His work as man's High Priest. Psalm 24:7-10 records heaven's reception for the victorious Saviour:

"Lift up your heads, O ye gates; and be ye lift up, ye everlasting doors; and the King of glory shall come in.

"Who is this King of glory? The Lord strong and mighty, the Lord mighty in battle.

"Lift up your heads, O ye gates; even lift them up, ye everlasting doors; and the King of glory shall come in.

"Who is this King of glory? The Lord of hosts, he is the King of glory. Selah."

With Christ's triumphant entrance into heaven, its inhabitants began the ten-day inauguration ceremonies for the victorious Saviour. Triumphantly He returned to finish the work He had successfully initiated on earth. He had lived a perfect human life as a substitute for the one that man found it impossible to live. He had died a sacrificial death for the sinful human race. Now, armed with these merits, He was ready to plead before God in behalf of sinners. His life and death on earth validated His authority to ask for forgiveness for mankind's crime.

When Jesus ascended to heaven, "a new and living way" opened whereby man could approach God and find forgiveness for his sin. The Jews who rejected His first advent found that their former means of access to God no longer stood open. The ministration of types and shadows had ceased. To unbelievers the door had shut, because they had lost the knowledge of Christ as the true Sacrifice and only Mediator before God. Because of this, they were unable to receive the benefits of His mediation.

The condition of the unbelieving Jews illustrates the condition of the careless and unbelieving among professed Christians, who remain willingly ignorant of the work of the High Priest.

In the typical service, when the high priest entered the holy places, all Israel gathered about the sanctuary. Solemnly they humbled their souls before God that they might receive pardon for their sins and not be "cut off" from the congregation.

Certain situations in the typical service called for the priest to apply the blood of the sin offering upon the horns of the altar of incense and sprinkle it seven times before the veil which separated the first apartment from the second. Thus the substitutionary death of the sinner through the offering of blood satisfied the holy law. Simultaneously the incense, like a fragrant cloud, ascended over the camp of Israel. In this representation mankind learned that God was to be approached by blood and incense.

It is an amazing fact that Christ died not only for believers, but for everyone whether or not he accepts His sacrifice. For the repentant sinner, Christ offers in the holy places not only His blood—signifying that He paid humanity's death penalty—but the merits of His righteousness. Christ died for two classes of people—repentant and unrepentant sinners—but He offers the incense of His perfect character only to believers.

In the daily ministrations the priest presented before God the blood of the sin offering. In the same manner, Christ pleads His blood before the Father in behalf of sinners, and presents before Him as well the fragrance of His own righteousness, the prayers of penitent believers.

Jesus, as the High Priest that Aaron and his descendants represented, entered once into the presence of God to make atonement. The Apostle Paul described this act in Hebrews 9:11, 12: "But Christ being come an high priest of good things to come, by a greater and more perfect tabernacle, not made with hands, that is to say, not of this building; neither by the blood of goats and calves, but by his own blood he entered in once into the holy place, having obtained eternal redemption for us."

Just as the human priest offered blood and incense, Christ presented His blood and the incense of His righteousness. With His sacrificial death and His perfect life, He atones for the sins of spiritual Israel.

What did Jesus do for you in the first apartment of the heavenly sanctuary?

Did He take the sins of unborn generations into the holy places with Him? Doubtless He did, for He entered but once into the "Holiest of all."

In patriarchal times the priest completed atonement in a day. In the Levitical period it took a year. But in the gospel age the process of atonement covers an era of many years. The Sin Bearer bore all the sins of the world—past, present, and future—on the cross. His righteousness stands available for all who accept His offer of salvation, for earth has no sin which Heaven cannot cover.

Paul summarized the value of Christ's sacrifice in Hebrews 9:23-28: "It was therefore necessary that the patterns of things in the heavens should be purified with these; but the heavenly things themselves with better sacrifices than these. For Christ is not entered into the holy places made with hands, which are the figures of the true; but into heaven itself, now to appear in the presence of God for us: nor yet that he should offer himself often, as the high priest entereth into the holy place every year with blood of others; for then must he often have suffered since the foundation of the world: but now once in the end of the world hath he appeared to put away sin by the sacrifice of himself. And as it is appointed unto men once to die, but after this the judgment: so Christ was once offered to bear the sins of many; and unto them that look for him shall he appear the second time without sin unto salvation."

Christ, after ascending to heaven, began His intercessory work in the first apartment of the heavenly sanctuary. There He pleaded His merits and right to make atonement for humanity. There He pleaded His death on the cross and His righteous life as a sacrifice for sin. He offered eternal life to all who would accept Him as their Saviour.

The daily sacrificial service in the court had its counterpart in the first apartment. As the priest killed the morning and evening lamb on the altar of burnt offering in the court, the incense ascended to God from the altar within. Thus, as the altar in the court typified the *continual atonement* of Christ, the altar before the most holy pointed to Christ's *perpetual intercession* before God.

The two supporting services quieted the demands of the law beyond the veil. The guilty had paid with his life through the Substitute, and the righteous character of the Saviour met the claims of the law.

As Mediator, Jesus was able to accomplish man's redemption, but at an incomprehensible price. The sinless Son of God was condemned for sin in which He had no part in order that man, through repentance and faith, might be justified by the righteousness of Christ, in which man had no part. Christ receives upon Himself the guilt of man's violations of the divine law. He lays His own perfection of character upon all who receive Him by faith and return to their allegiance to God.

The Book of Revelation gives a dramatic insight into the divine High Priest's ministry in the holy places of the heavenly sanctuary. While most of the Bible records historical events, the Book of Revelation reveals action going on today. All the themes of the Bible meet and end in Revelation. The book's stirring word pictures and figurative language portray events occurring on earth as well as in heaven.

The author of the Book of Hebrews states that "by his own blood he [Christ] entered in once into the holy place." (Hebrews 9:12.) John the revelator had a vision in which he "saw seven golden candlesticks; and in the midst of the seven candlesticks one like unto the Son of man, clothed with a garment down to the foot, and girt about the paps with a golden girdle." Revelation 1:12, 13. Obviously Christ was then ministering in the holy place of the heavenly sanctuary. Verses 14-16 give a further description of Christ as Priest: "His head and his hairs were white like wool, as white as snow; and his eyes were as a flame of fire; and his feet like unto fine brass, as if they burned in a furnace; and his voice as the sound of many waters. And he had in his right hand seven stars: and out of his mouth went a sharp twoedged sword: and his countenance was as the sun shineth in his strength."

The heavenly Priest identified Himself as Christ when He stated, "I am the first and the last: I am he that liveth, and was dead; and, behold, I am alive for evermore, Amen; and have the keys of hell and of death." Revelation 1:17, 18.

For eighteen hundred years Christ ministered in the holy place in heaven. John's vision included a brief summary of church history during the nearly two millenniums. Revelation 3:7, 8 mentions an open door, the way into the second compartment, associating it with the period of the church of Philadelphia, which some church historians believe to reach from 1798 to about 1846. The twenty-three-hundred-day prophecy of Daniel 8:14 pinpoints the time precisely to the Day of Atonement in 1844—October 22—when the longest specific time prophecy contained in the Bible came to an end. (See chapter 24.)

Although Christ's ministration continued in the first apartment of the sanctuary for eighteen centuries and He pleaded His blood in behalf of penitent believers and secured their pardon and acceptance with the Father, yet their sins still remained upon the books of record. As in the Hebrew sanctuary service, there existed a process to remove the symbolic collection of sin from heaven's sanctuary—a ceremony which began when the twenty-three-hundred-day prophecy ended. Then, as foretold by the Old Testament prophet Daniel, the High Priest entered the most holy compartment to perform the last division of His solemn mission, the cleansing of the sanctuary. (This theme will be more fully discussed in later chapters.)

# 6

# The Covenants

HOW A SINFUL being can be declared righteous before the perfect law of God is a problem that has troubled thinking men down through the ages. But to grasp the full meaning of the plan of salvation, one must have a knowledge of the covenants, agreements God established between Himself and man.

"Covenant" is a term which the legal profession holds in high esteem. Probably no other word used in law denotes more profoundly the rights and privileges of the individual. Although the word *contract* has largely replaced *covenant* in common usage, the latter remains the more revered and respected term. These two synonymous words—*covenant* and *contract*—make up half of the two great branches of jurisprudence—torts and contracts.

Covenants fall into the classifications of dependent, concurrent, and independent, as well as absolute. According to *Black's Legal Dictionary*, "the first depends on the prior performance of some act, or condition, and, until the condition is performed, the other party is not liable to an action on his covenant. In the second, mutual acts are to be performed at the same time; and if one party is ready, and offers to perform his part, and the other neglects or refuses to perform his, he who is ready and offers has fulfilled his engagement, and may maintain an action for the default of the other, though it is not certain that either is obliged to do the first act. The third sort is where either party may recover damages from the other for the injuries he may have received by a breach of the covenants in his favor; and it is no excuse for the defendant to allege a breach of the covenants on the part of the plaintiff." "An absolute covenant is one which is not qualified or limited by any condition."

Perhaps a more detailed classification can be reached by listing them, such as in the following manner:

1. Command
2. Promise
3. Agreement

The preceding gives a simple arrangement that includes all covenants in a legal and logical manner, whether for jurisprudence or Biblical interpretation. When considering covenants individually, one should determine first which type it is in order to comprehend it fully, because it is obviously important to know if he is dealing with a promise, a command, or an agreement.

The everlasting covenant is a *promised* covenant, entered into by God and Christ before the earth's creation. "In hope of eternal life, which God, that cannot lie, promised before the world began." Titus 1:2. Under it Christ promised to take the punishment and restore man to a correct relationship with God the Father should Satan overcome humanity. Solemnly they clasped hands as Christ took an oath not to change His mind about becoming man's Priest and Mediator. (See Psalm 89:34 and Hebrews 7:21.)

He would become man's substitute both for sin and for righteousness. Christ repeated the covenant to Adam, Abraham, Isaac, and Noah. It is the only covenant that provides for man's salvation. Under its terms, Christ would become part of the human race and through His merits gain humanity's entrance into heaven. Man had nothing to do with the compact, for he did not even exist when the Godhead formulated it.

Of the many *commanded* types of covenants mentioned in the Scriptures, by far the most prominent and important is the Ten Commandment covenant given at Sinai. "And he declared unto you his covenant, which he commanded you to perform, even ten commandments; and he wrote them upon two tables of stone." Deuteronomy 4:13. Specifically declared to be a covenant in many other Biblical references, it is God's law, an outline of His perfect character. (See Exodus 34:28; Deuteronomy 9:9, 11, 15; 29:1; Psalm 111:9.)

The Ten Commandments present the only standard of righteousness acceptable to God. God commands obedience to the contract, with death as the alternative. Man must demonstrate perfect compliance in order to meet its terms of "obey and live." Otherwise, it is a document of death to every created being.

Although God's commandments have existed throughout eternity, the Godhead presented them in a different form after the fall of Adam to meet man's needs in his new condition. Adam knew the law, as did Abraham, Noah, and all the patriarchs. Had Israel remembered its principles, they would never have gone into slavery in Egypt. During those long years of slavery, Israel had lost sight of their responsibilities to God and their fellowmen. Therefore, in awful grandeur, God and Christ together pronounced the Ten Commandments from Mount Sinai.

God also gave another covenant at Sinai called the "old covenant," so named because the blood which ratified it was shed before that of the new covenant, the latter ratified by Christ's death. Both covenants belong to the *agreement* type. At Sinai, God covenanted to be Israel's invisible King and to lead them into the earthly Canaan. They agreed to accept His rulership. Israel came into a close relationship with God and were incorporated as a church and nation under His government. The old covenant resulted in the only theocracy—a government with God at its head—the world has ever known.

On the other hand, the new covenant is a plan to lead the redeemed into the heavenly Canaan. It is the part of the everlasting covenant that began when the meaningful ministry of the earthly sanctuary ended. Like the ancient Hebrews, Christians promise to serve God and accept His rulership.

God gave both covenants. Neither of them was a covenant of works. Both had a sanctuary service with a priest, sabbaths, holy days, and ordinances. The old covenant given at Sinai revealed Christ as the true sacrifice for sin. The mystic types and symbols disclosed tracings of the great I AM. They depicted in unmistakable terms the plan of salvation. The earthly service was a striking visual aid, teaching the people daily the plan of atonement of the heavenly sanctuary.

Then, at the cross, type met antitype, actuality replaced symbols. The old covenant gave way to the new. Man no longer needed the shadowy symbols of the earthly service. Christ stood revealed as the Saviour of a fallen world. The ordinances and services of the Tabernacle terminated. They are what was symbolically nailed to the cross, not the law of God, as some claim. The commanded covenant was a separate one, revealing God's character.

The purpose of the law has ever been to reveal to man his need for a Saviour. It reveals sin and confronts the conscience, causing the sinner to feel his need of Christ as an atoning sacrifice for sin. The gospel recognizes the power and immutability of the law. In Romans 7:7, Paul declares, "I had not known sin, but by the law."

The Ten Commandments serve as the basis for all of

God's covenants, yet they form a separate entity. Similarly, the principles of freedom are the basis for the United States Constitution. One can abolish the Constitution, yet the principles of freedom remain eternal and changeless. The new covenant has supplanted the old, but its foundation principles—the Ten Commandments—exist forever. They cannot be done away with.

The Apostle Paul in Hebrews 8:6 says that the new covenant has more to offer to the believer than the old one: "But now hath he obtained a more excellent ministry, by how much also he is the mediator of a better covenant, which was established upon better promises."

## PROMISES OF GOD

| OLD COVENANT | NEW COVENANT |
|---|---|
| Good Promises | "Better Promises" |
| Earthly Church and Nation Under God | Heavenly Church and Nation Under God |
| Deliverance From Egypt | Deliverance From Sin |
| Earthly Canaan | Heavenly Canaan |
| Earthly Sanctuary | Heavenly Sanctuary |
| Earthly Jerusalem | Heavenly (New) Jerusalem |
| Earthly Priests | Heavenly Priests |
| | Eternal Life |
| Mortality | Immortality |

Both of the covenants were promises given by God. While the old covenant assured the possession of an earthly Canaan and an earthly Jerusalem, with a temporal inheritance, the new covenant pledged a land and city at first based in heaven, then later on a restored earth, whose inhabitants will have eternal life.

Through the merits of Christ the salvation of man has remained unchanged in all ages. He has pledged His promise to help man escape from eternal death under the terms of the everlasting covenant.

In the old dispensation men looked forward through faith to the promised Messiah. But Christians today live after the Messiah's first coming and await His return to the earth. Yet the fact remains that the obedience of modern Israel is no better than that of ancient Israel. Modern man's moral and spiritual nature has not improved. Our natures are still as "filthy rags." Only Christ can make up for humanity's imperfections. He has promised His followers that He will make them "perfect through the blood of the everlasting covenant." (Hebrews 13:20, 21.)

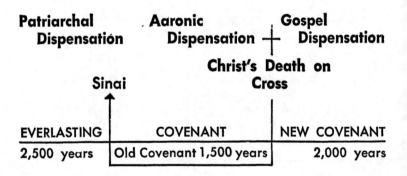

# THE TWO COVENANTS

|  | Old | New |
|---|---|---|
| **Type** | Agreement | Agreement |
| **Between** | God and Israel (literal) | God and Israel (spiritual) |
| **Benefit to** | Israel (literal) | Israel (spiritual) |
| **Duration** | Temporary and provisional<br>1,500 years | Changeless and eternal |
| **Terms** | Obey and live | Obey and live |
| **Basis** | God's law | God's law |
| **Sanctuary** | Earthly | Heavenly |
| **Priests** | Human | Divine—human |
| **Reward** | Earthly Canaan | Heavenly Canaan |
| **Nature** | Faulty (blood of beasts)<br>Sinful priests | Faultless (blood of Christ)<br>Sinless Priest |
| **Testator** | Animals | Christ |
| **Mediator** | Human priest | Divine Priest |
| **Law** | Ordinances (provisional) | Ten Commandments |
| **Promises** | Of God | Of God |
| **Ratified** | Blood (death) of animals | Blood (death) of Christ |
| **Purpose** | To point the world to the new covenant. | To fulfill the pledge God and Christ made from eternity. |
|  | To lead literal Israel to the earthly Canaan. | To lead spiritual Israel to the heavenly Canaan. |
|  | To teach Christ's atoning work. | To complete the atonement of God and man. |
|  | To reveal the immutability of the law. | To reveal the immutability of the law. |
|  | To demonstrate the sinner's need for a Substitute and a Priest. | To demonstrate that Christ is all the sinner needs to be saved. |
|  |  | To ratify the everlasting covenant. |

# 7

# Atonement in Patriarchal Times

ADAM'S SIN placed humanity on Satan's side. The first man had come from the hand of the Creator perfect in every respect, with no tendency toward evil. Since Adam was the first created being on earth and all humanity has descended from him, he in essence contained the entire human race within him. Thus one can say that when Adam sinned, all mankind sinned. All have inherited his alienation from God the Father.

Adam's fall in the Garden of Eden plunged the human race into sin, but Christ drank the bitter cup of suffering and death in the Garden of Gethsemane so that His believers would not perish, but would have access to immortality. In fact, humanity still lives under the death sentence because of Adam's transgression, but the everlasting covenant has delayed the penalty.

God did not pardon Adam and Eve as soon as they sinned. Instead He granted a stay of execution, pending Christ's mediatorial work in behalf of the condemned race. Humanity would have a second chance by virtue of the atonement.

Although God did not immediately free Adam from the death sentence, He did reveal the entire plan of salvation, the atonement, to the first man. Adam understood the part Christ would play under the terms of the everlasting covenant in restoring the human race to oneness with God. With unutterable sorrow, he comprehended the effect his sin had upon his descendants and the world. Regretfully he acknowledged the fact that the Son of God must die because of his transgression. But as angels drove the guilty pair from the Garden of Eden, hope mingled with despair. They recognized their salvation in the coming of the Messiah, who would reconcile God and man to each other.

To strengthen and to impress the story of the fall upon men's minds, God ordained the altar service—the visual aid of the Bible. Types and prophecy in the patriarchal dispensation went hand in hand, to keep before the race the great truths relative to God and His amazing love for them. They were God's educational tools, telling about the coming Messiah, who would be man's substitute for sin and righteousness. These two tools have ever been the signposts directing the fallen sons and daughters of Adam to the atonement so freely offered.

Christ, in counsel with His Father, established the system of sacrificial offerings, that death, instead of being visited upon the transgressor at once, should be transferred to a victim which would prefigure the great and perfect offering of the Son of God.

The bleeding victim consumed in the fire on the altar illustrated Adam's teaching, deepening the impression it made. The impressive altar service formed the basis for a system of worship ordained by God and practiced by believers for twenty-five hundred years. The Book of Genesis concisely covers this period.

God revealed to such ancient personalities as Adam, Abel, Seth, Enoch, Noah, Abraham, and especially Moses that the ceremonial offerings pointed to Christ. Through these symbols they became more aware of Christ and believed more deeply in Him.

God ordained the offerings to constantly remind His followers of the fearful separation which sin had made between

God and man. Through Christ the communication cut off because of Adam's rebellion reopened between God and the sinner. To illustrate the fact, God instituted mediatorial worship. Although Christ has always served as the true Mediator or Priest between man and God, God also used human intercessors, representing Christ, prior to His incarnation. He had not yet put on the cloak of humanity, and so could not be priest to intercede for His people. In order to be priest between God and man, Christ must be both man and God. Only by having such a duality of nature could He have complete access to both.

Before the time of Moses each man served as the priest of his own household, the priesthood being regarded as the birthright of the eldest son. A household might consist of a large gathering of relatives and servants, all living together in a group. Most of God's people were nomadic, carrying their possessions and driving their flocks with them. Wherever they camped, they erected an altar. Morning and evening found the family in prayer at the foot of the altar, led by the father, who acted as the priest, the mediator of the patriarchal dispensation.

In addition to his twice-daily worship, a person who had sinned could escape from his guilt only by a specific and exacting sacrificial service. With sorrow and contrition he went to the priest and confessed his guilt. In God's plan the sinner, upon confessing, became free from the sin, and it symbolically passed to the priest, who became his substitute. The transfer made the priest guilty of the sin confessed to him, thus absolving the sinner. The priest became the sin bearer and as such stood guilty before the law of God, which condemned him to die.

But the human priest could not die as the perfect sacrifice the law demanded, for he was also a sinner. He could not atone through his imperfect life for another human being. Because the priest was born in a race of beings alienated from God, he had to find a suitable substitute—a spotless lamb. The priest thus transferred the confessed sin onto the head of the animal and killed it. The innocent animal and its sacrificial death provided an atonement for the priest and sinner, but only when the penitent believer demonstrated his belief in the Saviour to come by his obedience to the sacrificial system.

"The sins of the people were transferred in figure to the officiating priest, who was a mediator for the people," one author has commented. "The priest could not himself become an offering for sin, and make an atonement with his life, for he was also a sinner. Therefore, instead of suffering death himself, he [the priest] killed a lamb without blemish; the penalty of sin was transferred to the innocent beast, which thus became his [the priest's] immediate substitute, and typified the perfect offering of Jesus Christ. Through the blood of this victim, man looked forward by faith to the blood of Christ which would atone for the sins of the world."—Ellen G. White, in *Signs of the Times,* March 14, 1878. (*Questions on Doctrine,* p. 669.)

The context seems to indicate that this statement applies to the patriarchal period. By noting the antecedents of the pronouns *he* and *him,* the reader will see that they refer to the priest and that it is the priest who kills the lamb as his immediate substitute.

This quotation makes clear the principle contained in several Scriptural references which indicate that Christ died as both Lamb and Priest. In addition, it points unmistakably to the fact that the priest must symbolically die, and that Christ, the fulfillment of the priest symbol, died at Calvary. Hebrews 9:11, 12 states that Christ acted both as Priest and as Victim. He offered Himself to God without blemish.

Adam's tempter had used guile in approaching the guilty pair. Satan had tricked and hypnotized Eve and had unduly influenced Adam. Because of this intrigue, Deity determined that man should have a second chance, a second probation.

God offered atonement during the patriarchal dispensation for the condemned human race. The patriarchal dispensation may be compared with the court of the Hebrew sanctuary. As the service in the court prepared for the ceremony of bringing blood and incense into the first and second apartments, so the patriarchal dispensation established the foundation for the development of the true atonement through Christ.

The ceremony of the altar service demonstrated two great principles of God's love—justice and mercy. It offered mercy to the repentant sinner, whose sin and death penalty were transferred to the priest and then to the lamb, which became the priest's substitute; and it revealed justice by satisfying the broken law of God with the lamb's blood.

Atonement in the patriarchal dispensation, as in all periods of time, came through a priest offering a sacrifice as a substitute for his death, that is, the death of the *priest*. It must be kept in mind that it was the priest who should die in the sinner's place.

Cain and Abel represented the two great classes of people down through the stream of time. Abel demonstrated acceptance of the atonement provided for his salvation. By his obedience to the sacrificial service of his age, he acknowledged his sin and revealed his need of the substitutionary atonement of the coming Messiah. In the dying agonies of the sacrificial animal, he saw symbolized the "Lamb of God, which taketh away the sin of the world." (John 1:29.)

Cain, on the other hand, illustrates the class who do not

accept Christ's atonement. Cain was not an atheist, since he believed in God. He brought an offering, but he saw no need for a sacrificial animal. He did not accept the fact that there is no remission of sin without death—a fact depicted through the shedding of the animal's blood. Cain wanted to be saved, but he believed that his way was as good as the one God had outlined. He offered as his sacrifice, his personal fruits in place of the unblemished lamb, which pointed to Christ. Cain's sacrifice attempted to cover up the atonement. He presented a counterfeit religion, a religion of earning God's favor through meritorious deeds. Cain refused to acknowledge his need of a Redeemer. To him such an act represented dependence and humiliation.

At every altar, in every sacrifice, God's people saw Christ as the Sin Bearer, the Lamb, the Priest, the Holy Substitute, the coming Messiah. Christ, the true Priest of the house of Israel, would bear their sins, make atonement, and die as a result.

Because of His faultlessness, Christ could and did die at the cross as man's Substitute. He was both offerer and offering at the cross, and died as both Lamb and Priest.

Why the old dispensation required sacrificial offerings has puzzled many. They have questioned why the patriarchs needed to lead so many bleeding victims to the altar. But God wanted to keep one great truth before man and imprint it upon his mind—"without shedding of blood is no remission." (Hebrews 9:22.) Divine justice recognized that the alienation between God and man could be permanently ended only through the death of the one who had started it—man. The dying sacrifice reminded man that Christ—symbolized by the lamb —would die in humanity's place.

Far from being a distasteful practice, the patriarchal altar service was impressive and vibrant. God used it as a thought-provoking visual aid to teach men about the atoning sacrifice of Christ. Wherever Abraham pitched his tent, he set up an altar nearby and called all within his encampment to the morning and evening sacrifice. Passersby often became interested in the display and inquired about its purpose.

When Abraham moved on, the altar remained as a reminder of the patriarch and the worship of God. In succeeding years roving Canaanites who had received instruction at the altar thought of Abraham and of Christ's mediatorial role. Whenever travelers came upon such an altar, they knew who had passed that way before. Some would even repair the altar and worship there the true God of heaven.

The patriarchal ceremonial offering has great lessons for us today. This service perpetually reminded Adam and his posterity of their guilt. In addition, it allowed men to penitentially acknowledge their sin and demonstrate their dependence upon Christ as their atonement. The act of taking life gave the patriarchs a deeper and more perfect sense of their transgression, which no one but the Son of God could expiate. No personal penitent acts of man can possibly atone for the transgression of the law which the race had committed. Today, as then, our only hope lies in the Saviour's life of perfect obedience to all of God's commandments and His sacrificial death on the cross.

# 8

# Melchizedek, a Symbol of Christ

MUCH MYSTERY surrounds Melchizedek and his role in Bible history and the atonement. "Thou art a priest for ever after the order of Melchizedek," the psalmist quotes God the Father as saying to Christ. (Psalm 110:4.) For emphasis, the author of the Book of Hebrews uses the statement seven times. The Bible, however, provides little detail about Melchizedek. The first mention of him is in Genesis. Because this book deals with twenty-five centuries, it often presents only the briefest accounts of events and important people. Moses, the author of Genesis, described Melchizedek with three verses: "And Melchizedek king of Salem brought forth bread and wine: and he was the priest of the most high God. And he blessed him, and said, Blessed be Abram of the most high God, possessor of heaven and earth: and blessed be the most high God, which hath delivered thine enemies into thy hand. And he gave him tithes of all." Genesis 14:18-20.

The reader can derive several important points from the brief description. First, he is king of Salem, a village later to become Jerusalem, the Hebrews' holy city. The name "Salem" comes from the Hebrew word *shalem* (shaw-lame) meaning "peaceful" and is akin to *shalam* (shaw-lam), a prime root word meaning "completed, to be safe, to make peace, to be at peace."

Eight hundred years before David's coronation, Melchizedek, priest of God, had made Salem his home. Christ in a similar manner will be crowned as King of righteousness and King of peace and will have the New Jerusalem, heaven's Holy City, as the capital of His domain. His kingdom will last forever, and its subjects will consist of those saved under the terms of the Abrahamic covenant.

The Bible depicts Melchizedek as a "priest of the most high God." Although he lived in patriarchal times, he apparently was not a typical patriarchal priest like Abraham, because Abraham accepted his blessing and paid tithe to him. The analogy between Christ and this "priest of the most high God" is obvious. Christ also served as Priest of the Most High God while He lived among men, and even now ministers in the sanctuary in heaven. God assigned both priests their roles in a special manner, unlike the selection of either the patriarchal or the Levitical priest.

The Bible does not designate the kind of sanctuary Melchizedek served in, but it clearly identifies Christ's sanctuary, referring to it as the "Holiest of all," the "greater and more perfect tabernacle, not made with hands."

Both Melchizedek and Christ represented God on earth. Melchizedek in his day was the voice of God in the world, the advocate of God the Father. Similarly Christ came to dwell among men in order to depict the personality of the Father. Mankind had largely lost sight of God and His purpose during the four thousand years of sin that separated the first Adam from the second Adam. But Christ came to give a correct picture of God and His love. When the disciples asked, "Shew us the Father," He alone could answer, "He that hath seen me hath seen the Father." (John 14:8, 9.)

Moses, the gospel writer of Genesis, mentions just four events out of Melchizedek's life. Accordingly they must be highlights in his existence:

1. He came to meet Abraham's army.
2. He brought bread and wine.
3. He blessed Abraham.
4. He accepted Abraham's tithe.

In considering these events, one must keep in mind that the redeemed will be saved under the terms of the Abrahamic covenant. Abraham, father of the faithful, has his spiritual army of followers, just as he once had a literal army in Melchizedek's day. As one considers Christ and Melchizedek, he finds analogies in Christ's life to these four activities described in Genesis.

As Melchizedek came forth to greet Abraham's victorious armies, so Christ at His second coming will come out of the heavenly sanctuary to bless the redeemed—Abraham's spiritual army—who are saved under the terms of the Abrahamic covenant.

When Melchizedek greeted the victorious forces of Abraham, he "brought forth bread and wine." (Genesis 14:18.) In symbolic terms, the act carried deep significance with reference to the atonement. The "bread and wine" Melchizedek offered to Abraham resemble Christ's flesh and blood, for He declared, "Whoso eateth my flesh, and drinketh my blood, hath eternal life." John 6:54. As Melchizedek offered Abraham and his followers the "bread and wine," so Christ offers atonement to the fallen descendants of Adam. Christ's life of perfection (His righteous body or flesh) and His sacrificial death (the blood) make the only reconciliation God can accept. "He that eateth my flesh, and drinketh my blood, dwelleth in me, and I in him. As the living Father hath sent me, and I live by the Father: so he that eateth me, even he shall live by me." John 6:56, 57.

Abraham's paying tithes to Melchizedek indicates that

although Abraham was the father of Israel, the main repository of the knowledge of God in the world, the priest held a higher position. Furthermore, the "priest of the most high God" blessed Abraham, something generally done by a superior. In bestowing the benediction upon Abraham, Melchizedek acknowledged God as the source of his strength and the author of Abraham's victory.

The next mention of Melchizedek occurs in Psalm 110:4. As the psalm opens, it portrays a dialogue. "The Lord said unto my Lord, Sit thou at my right hand, until I make thine enemies thy footstool." Obviously this depicts a prophetic conversation between God and Christ. Jesus in Matthew 22:41-45, Mark 12:35-37, and Luke 20:41-43 says the psalm refers to the Christ. God invites Christ to sit at His right hand until He subdues His enemies.

The verb *sit*, as used here, denotes power, to occupy a place or seat in an official capacity, as a king sits on the throne. Christ, in His capacity of Priest of the Most High God, now occupies His position at the right hand of God.

To become a true priest, mediating between man and God, Christ had to become a man. A priest must be the arbiter between the two parties at variance. He must understand fully the problems involved on both sides. In Christ's case, He had to know the views of man and God. Under the covenant of mercy, Christ promised to become Priest and Mediator. He swore to keep His word by an oath and a promise, the two immutable things mentioned in Hebrews 6:18. Psalm 110:4 strongly states it again: "The Lord hath sworn, and will not repent, Thou art a priest for ever after the order of Melchizedek."

Paul used the Book of Hebrews to present the priesthood of Christ. Significantly, he did not mention the sacrificial lamb in the epistle, only the Priest. He directed his discourse to his fellow Jews, well versed in the Hebrew sanctuary service and acquainted with the priest, his background, and duties.

The apostle recorded Christ's call to the priesthood in Hebrews 5:6, 7, and in verse 1 of this chapter he reaffirmed the fact that all priests must come from among men—a situation true of the patriarchal priest, the Aaronic priest, Melchizedek, and Christ. "For every high priest taken from among men is ordained for men." "And no man taketh this honour unto himself." Hebrews 5:1, 4.

As God chose and called Melchizedek to be priest, so God called Jesus to the priesthood. The apostle cited Psalm 110 in Hebrews to support the idea: "Thou art a priest for ever after the order of Melchisedec." Verse 6.

Christ came neither from the family of Aaron nor the tribe of Levi, but sprang from the tribe of Judah. The Bible makes no mention of the tribe of Judah ever being associated with the Aaronic priesthood. Christ belonged to a higher order of priesthood, but He patterned His entire life of service after the Aaronic tabernacle system. From the time of His birth to the hour of His death on Passover day, to His rest in the grave on redemption Sabbath, to His resurrection on wave-sheaf day as the antitype of the firstfruits of the Lord, Jesus fulfilled all the types and prophecies foreshadowed in the Jewish typical service. As a final confirmation of His role, Heaven anointed Him to His work in the heavenly sanctuary on Pentecost.

The mysteries surrounding the person of Melchizedek appear unfathomable. Some declare that he was God the Father. Others say that he was Christ or the Holy Spirit. In order to determine his true nature, the Bible student must review the meager details available.

What did Moses call him? King and priest (both offices held by men).

What did David call him? Priest (all priests chosen from men).

What did Paul declare him to be? A man. (Hebrews 7:4.)

One may conclude then that Melchizedek was a man, who served both as king of Salem and as a priest of God of a higher category than that of the patriarchal priesthood Abraham belonged to. He acted as the voice of God on earth for his day.

Surely the Old Testament symbols of atonement would be incomplete without Melchizedek as priest, for his position reveals the role of Christ in a way that neither the patriarchal nor Levitical priest could do. While these priests came to office by virtue of their family, and someone succeeded them after their death, the Bible describes Melchizedek as being "without father, without mother, without descent, having neither beginning of days, nor end of life, but made like unto the Son of God; [who] abideth a priest continually." (Hebrews 7:3.)

It was absolutely essential that a typical priest such as Melchizedek appear before Christ's birth, because Jesus obviously was not a Priest of the earthly tabernacle. Yet in type and prophecy the Bible presents Him as Priest. Being called "after the order of Melchizedek" solved the dilemma and helped explain the nature of Christ's priesthood. Both Christ and Melchizedek were called in a special manner by God.

Doubtless inspiration intended to leave Melchizedek cloaked with mystery. The Bible says little about him, yet his importance is obvious. Perhaps if one stripped the aura of the unknown from Melchizedek, he would also reduce the wonder of Christ's incarnation. Unanswerable questions surround Christ and Melchizedek which finite man cannot explain. But we do know that he was "the priest of the most high God."

## 9

# The Sanctuary Throughout the Bible

BEGINNING with Genesis and ending with Revelation, every section of the Bible develops and enlarges the theme of atonement. The Bible is essentially a revelation of how God provided for man's salvation through the service of the heavenly sanctuary. It points out that the reconciliation of man to God, and God to man, results from the substitutionary role of Jesus as Sacrifice and High Priest.

The first book of the Bible hints at the sanctuary through God's promise of redemption. "I will put enmity between thee and the woman, and between thy seed and her seed," He said. "It shall bruise thy head, and thou shalt bruise his heel." Genesis 3:15. In the simple patriarchal worship service with the family altar, the priest, and the lamb, the sinner approached God through a substitute. The sanctuary was in embryo form.

The books of Exodus, Leviticus, and Deuteronomy portray the development of the sanctuary in a physical form. In Exodus 25:8, God said, "And let them make me a sanctuary; that I may dwell among them." God showed Moses a model of His dwelling place and gave detailed instructions about the construction of the Tabernacle, listing articles of furniture, the clothing of the priests, and the order of the service to be conducted. More than forty chapters deal with the erection of the wilderness sanctuary and its symbolic worship.

The historical accounts of the Hebrew kings record that the physical sanctuary became enlarged. The Temple in Jerusalem replaced the portable tent structure. This magnificent structure occupied one sixth of the sacred city. Solomon received this promise from God: "Concerning this house which thou art building, if thou wilt walk in my statutes, and execute my judgments, and keep all my commandments to walk in them; then will I perform my word with thee, which I spake unto David thy father: and I will dwell among the children of Israel, and will not forsake my people Israel." 1 Kings 6: 12, 13.

The psalms exalted the sanctuary. Poetic eloquence praised and extolled God's love revealed in the atonement. Said David, "Blessed is he whose transgression is forgiven, whose sin is covered. Blessed is the man unto whom the Lord imputeth not iniquity, and in whose spirit there is no guile." Psalm 32:1, 2.

"They have seen thy goings, O God; even the goings of my God, my King, in the sanctuary." Psalm 68:24.

"Thy way, O God, is in the sanctuary: who is so great a God as our God?" Psalm 77:13.

"Praise ye the Lord. Praise God in his sanctuary: praise him in the firmament of his power. Praise him for his mighty acts: praise him according to his excellent greatness." Psalm 150:1, 2.

The major prophets discuss the sanctuary desecrated and destroyed. God's faithful servants bemoan the ravaging of the Temple and the blasphemy of impious hands that build gods of wood, silver, and stone.

"To what purpose is the multitude of your sacrifices unto me? saith the Lord: I am full of the burnt offerings of rams, and the fat of fed beasts; and I delight not in the blood of bullocks, or of lambs, or of he goats." "How is the faithful city become an harlot! it was full of judgment; righteousness lodged in it; but now murderers." Isaiah 1:11, 21.

"Wherefore, as I live, saith the Lord God; Surely, because thou hast defiled my sanctuary with all thy detestable things, and with all thine abominations, therefore will I also diminish thee; neither shall mine eye spare, neither will I have any pity." Ezekiel 5:11.

Daniel mentions a counterfeiting of the sanctuary. The opening verses of the Book of Daniel tell how Israel's enemies seized the sacred Temple vessels to use in the service of idolatry. Babylon persecuted and enslaved those who worshiped in the true sanctuary. Some of its leaders had the prophet himself thrown into a lions' den. God miraculously preserved him and revealed to him future events. In vision, Daniel saw that a spurious system of worship would develop in the world. For a time most men would not have a correct understanding of the doctrine of the heavenly sanctuary. Its worshipers would be hunted, tortured, and put to death. A rival religious system would arise, and its leader would attempt to gain great power. Says the prophet, "Yea, he magnified himself even to the prince of the host, and by him the daily sacrifice was taken away, and the place of his sanctuary was cast down." Daniel 8:11. But the false system would finally collapse. Salvation through the heavenly sanctuary would triumph according to God's promise. Even as literal oppressive Babylon faced eventual destruction, so spiritual Babylon would come to her end.

The minor prophets show the captivity of God's people turned and the sanctuary restored. God, His heart yearning with love, cried to His people, "Turn ye even to me with all your heart: . . . and turn unto the Lord your God: for he is gracious and merciful, slow to anger, and of great kindness, and repenteth him of the evil." Joel 2:12, 13.

73

The Hebrews rebuilt their sanctuary, and though unequal in magnificence to the first structure, it received far greater honor. "The glory of this latter house shall be greater than of the former, saith the Lord of hosts: and in this place will I give peace." Haggai 2:9. God Himself, the incarnate Christ, glorified the second Temple with His bodily presence.

In the New Testament, the Gospel writers reveal the antitype of the earthly, or Levitical, sanctuary, and the mission carried on in the court by the divine High Priest. The service of the sanctuary changed from the earth to heaven. The New Testament authors present four aspects of Christ's role. "Behold the Lamb of God, which taketh away the sin of the world," the Baptist cried. Anointed by the Holy Ghost, Jesus bore the accumulated guilt of all mankind to the altar on Golgotha and offered a perfect atoning sacrifice, Himself the Lamb, Himself the Priest. The veil of the Jewish sanctuary was ripped apart, and the service was transferred from earth to heaven. The risen Saviour in His glorified humanity stood at the right hand of God to plead His merits for those whom He had died to save.

In the Book of Acts the descent of the Holy Spirit on the day of Pentecost indicated the dedication of the sanctuary in heaven and the anointing of the divine High Priest for His work in its sacred apartments. The Comforter came to teach men of a new way to approach the Creator. Peter cried, "Repent and be baptized every one of you in the name of Jesus Christ for the remission of sins, and ye shall receive the gift of the Holy Ghost." Acts 2:38.

The Epistles explain the sanctuary symbolism and relate it to the life and mission of Christ. Christ's sacrifice on the cross stands revealed as the core of the Christian religion. "Much more then, being now justified by his blood, we shall be saved from wrath through him. For if, when we were enemies, we were reconciled to God by the death of his Son, much more, being reconciled, we shall be saved by his life. And not only so, but we also joy in God through our Lord Jesus Christ, by whom we have now received the atonement." Romans 5:9-11.

The Book of Hebrews is the greatest exposition on the sanctuary doctrine. It contrasts the sanctuary on earth with the one in heaven and compares the old and new covenants. But most important of all, it points out man's new Priest.

"But Christ being come an high priest of good things to come, by a greater and more perfect tabernacle, not made with hands, that is to say, not of this building; neither by the blood of goats and calves, but by his own blood entered in once into the holy place, having obtained eternal redemption for us." Hebrews 9:11, 12.

To understand the heavenly sanctuary, the author of Hebrews said, one must study closely the pattern that once existed on earth. He admonished spiritual Israel to avoid the pitfalls of unbelief into which literal Israel fell.

The Apostle John in the Book of Revelation provided the climax of the whole sanctuary story. He showed how the sanctuary in heaven functions. "Clothed with a garment down to the foot, and girt about the paps with a golden girdle" (Revelation 1:13), Christ ministers in the midst of the seven golden candlesticks. In his vision John saw a "Lamb as it had been slain" and an angel standing at the altar with a golden censer, offering "much incense" with the prayers of the saints. (Revelation 8:3.) Those portions of the Book of Daniel which were formerly sealed now stand revealed at "the time of the end." (Daniel 12:4.)

Jesus moves from the first apartment to the second, shutting one door and opening another. The counterfeit sanctuary prophesied by Daniel developed on earth, while the service in heaven advanced toward the day of judgment. Then Christ as Priest will remove His mediatorial robes and put on the garments of vengeance. He will leave the sanctuary escorted by all the holy angels, and will glorify and make immortal the redeemed. The lake of fire will consume Satan's evil hosts, for sin and sinners are to be no more.

"And I heard a great voice out of heaven saying, Behold, the tabernacle of God is with men, and he will dwell with them, and they shall be his people, and God himself shall be with them, and be their God." Revelation 21:3.

# 10

# The Jewish Era

NO STUDY of the atonement and its significance to man would be complete without taking into account the long years of slavery which Abraham's descendants endured. After the dark centuries God chose to reveal Himself through more symbols to the new nation gathered at the foot of Mount Sinai. Long had God waited to give His covenant to the world. Their bitter bondage in a strange country had prepared the Hebrews to accept God's invitation to come out of Egypt and throw off the shackles of oppression.

Unarmed, uneducated, and defenseless, they did not realize that they would conquer mighty armies and overwhelm great nations on their journey to the land of Canaan, the land promised to them through Abraham centuries before.

On two previous occasions, God had purposed to give the world a knowledge of the atonement through a people dedicated to Him. Adam and Eve, as the angels drove them from the Garden of Eden, received the promise of redemption and the Messiah. Each succeeding generation anticipated His coming. But the human race, even though little removed from creation, degenerated into such sin and licentiousness that God proposed to destroy the world and to start anew with faithful Noah.

Again He made the gracious offer of pardon and reconciliation, but mankind rejected it. Soon the patriarchs' descendants began building a refuge tower at Babel in defiance of God's promise to never allow a global flood again. They worshiped gods of metal and stone.

But God could not permit mankind to perish because of a lack of knowledge of His plan for their salvation. He had outlined the everlasting covenant to Adam and Noah. Now He transmitted it to Abraham. God planned for him to be the father of a nation. It would be a theocracy, ruled by God Himself. Over four hundred years had passed, but now the promise seemed about to be fulfilled. God would start anew with Israel, His chosen people.

God led an unpromising group out of Egypt on the first Passover night. Their long years of bondage had reduced them to a state possibly even worse than that of the American slave at the time of the Civil War. But, in spite of their lack of qualifications, they were the chosen ones for that period of earth's history.

Israel's mission had three aspects: They were to be the source of the world's knowledge of God, the channel through which the Messiah would come, and a witness for God before all nations.

God wanted to show what He could do with such a discouraging collection of human beings. Clearly, He had not chosen them because of their spiritual superiority, for He had said of them, "Not for thy righteousness, or for the uprightness of thine heart, dost thou go to possess their land." Deuteronomy 9:5. And in the next verse Moses said, "Understand therefore, that the Lord thy God giveth thee not this good land to possess it for thy righteousness; for thou art a stiffnecked people."

It now became necessary for God to reveal what He expected of them. In awe-inspiring grandeur at Sinai, God proclaimed the basic law of heaven and earth. Amid peals of thunder and flashes of lightning, God the Father and Christ in unison pronounced the law. Then, to show its immutability, the Lord wrote the commandments in stone with His own finger. Although in existence from eternity, the Decalogue was now presented in a form suited for fallen humanity.

Afraid for their lives, all Israel readily agreed to obey it. "All that the Lord hath spoken we will do," came their unanimous cry. They did not realize their inability to give the total obedience the law demanded. Since the decree had been to obey and live or disobey and die, they had no alternative.

At Mount Sinai Israel became a theocracy. Never before or since has God condescended to enter into an agreement with an actual nation on earth. Patiently God had waited 430 years to set up His government under the covenant He had made with Abraham. Now He proposed to be their King and lead them into Canaan. Israel agreed to be His people and to accept Him as their Ruler. They promised to render unquestioning obedience to the Lord. The possibility of becoming a great and wealthy nation under God certainly seemed worth any consideration, especially after their long years of bondage in Egypt.

But they could not comprehend that they had pledged themselves to an impossibility. They did not realize that sinful nature cannot obey a perfect law without Christ's atoning blood. They soon learned through sad experience that they had forfeited all right to the covenant promises. Quickly they reverted to idolatry and licentious practices.

The humiliating experience of worshiping the golden calf forced Israel to recognize that disobedience would never bring them the blessings of God. Now it became clear that they must perish in the Sinai wilderness and die for eternity, unreconciled to God. To avert such a calamity, Moses, as their human mediator, pleaded with God for mercy and pardon.

Mercy prevailed, but even then, over three thousand of the unrepentant died in the desert wastes, and all Israel stood guilty before God.

The incident exhibited the wonders of the everlasting covenant. If it had not been for this covenant, God would have had to destroy the human race without delay. After Israel's disgraceful fall, Moses again ascended Mount Sinai and met with God, who again imprinted the commandments in stone with His finger. Over the next year and a half, God communed with His servant from the most holy place of the Hebrew Tabernacle. From the Shekinah, overlooking the mercy seat, God presented the ceremonial law, which outlined the appointed method of worship until Christ's death on the cross. Moses wrote down its details in a book, trusting nothing to memory.

God designed the ritual of Hebrew worship to lead the minds of the condemned people to a knowledge of the plan of salvation. The ceremonies pointed out that the substitutionary life and death of Jesus provided reconciliation with God for every repentant sinner. Now humble and distrustful of themselves, the people came to appreciate the provisions of the covenant made with their ancestor Abraham. The sacrificial service kindled their faith and hope as they looked across the years to Christ's first coming and His provisions to free them from their sins.

The Tabernacle's dramatic portrayal of redemption taught them the love of God as nothing else could have done. All Israelites were actors in this great play. They found the sanctuary the center of all their activities. They knew that their actual existence depended on the work performed for them by the priests. Until the advent of the true High Priest the human mediators and animal sacrifices provided a means by which man might approach the Creator with his petitions and praise.

The details of the simple altar service of patriarchal times had grown dim in Israel's memory. Long years of slavery had caused them to forget God. Because of such conditions, God devised a more elaborate system to teach the marvelous plan of atonement. The earthly Tabernacle served as a giant visual aid where the people could daily see and study the working of the plan of salvation.

The Levitical sanctuary represented a continuation of the simple altar of patriarchal times when the head of the family became priest and mediator. Now the altar ceremony developed into a magnificent ritual. Instead of a priest for each family, the priesthood consisted of the males of the tribe of Levi. Only the sons of Aaron, however, officiated in the actual sacrificial service. The sacrifices and offerings grew in number and symbolisms, all of them pointing to the great I AM (Exodus 3:14), the one Mediator between God and man.

The one-day cycle of atonement of the days of the patriarchs now became so complicated that it took a year to achieve its completion. At all times some service was in progress in the Tabernacle. The sin offerings, the various peace offerings, the cleansing ceremonies, the sacrifice of the red heifer, and many other activities took place there constantly.

The altar of burnt offerings in the court illustrated the continuous sacrifice of Jesus, while the altar of incense in the first apartment, with its fire kindled by God, typified Christ's perpetual intercession for man.

All year long the priest symbolically took sins into the sanctuary, but at the close of the year, on the Day of Atonement, a special ceremony removed them, completing the cycle. The numerous rites *taught the people clearly that atonement is a process rather than a single act.*

The Day of Atonement caused the Hebrews to look ahead

81

to the final purification of the universe from sin and sinners and the end of the controversy between Christ and Satan.

The entire Jewish way of life revolved around the Tabernacle and its service. While God was their invisible King, the high priest acted as His representative on earth. He was the lawgiver, judge, and diagnostician, the only means of communication between man and God. Upon him rested the responsibility of pronouncing the death sentence or the right to live. He made the diagnosis of leprosy, from which there could be no reprieve.

God Himself gave Moses the plan to follow in the construction of the earthly sanctuary. He presented specific instructions about its size and shape. The structure and its furnishings would be "patterns of things in the heavens," "figures of the true." (Hebrews 9:23, 24.) The Tabernacle was the miniature representation of the heavenly temple, where Christ, man's High Priest, after offering His life as a sacrifice would minister in behalf of the sinner.

The Tabernacle was a magnificent structure and, although portable, was a building of outstanding beauty. The walls, of upright acacia boards set in silver sockets and well braced with pillars and connecting bars, had a gold overlay, giving the edifice the appearance of solid gold. The four layers of curtains forming the roof consisted of, first, an inner curtain of fine-quality linen in blue, scarlet, and purple with exquisite embroidered cherubim; second, a mohair covering; third, a curtain of rams' skins dyed red; and fourth, a layer of sealskin.

A curtain similar to the ceiling, inwrought with gold and silver threads portraying cherubim, divided the building into two chambers. The first apartment was called the holy place, and the second apartment the most holy place, after their counterparts in heaven.

A courtyard enclosed with hanging linens supported by pillars of brass surrounded the Tabernacle. The principal feature in the court was the altar of burnt offering. Made of burnished brass, it stood near the east entrance. There fire consumed the sacrifices, and the priest sprinkled the atoning blood upon the horns at each corner of the altar.

Several hundred years later the Jews built a permanent Temple on Mount Moriah. Envisioned by David and built by Solomon, the structure far surpassed the wilderness Tabernacle in beauty and splendor. Authorities have described it as having been garnished with precious stones and surrounded by spacious courts with magnificent approaches. Carved cedar and burnished gold lined the interior walls. Hangings and furnishings decorated it to make it a suitable emblem of the church of God on earth.

While the model on earth was an ingenious structure of great beauty, it paled into insignificance when compared with the sanctuary in heaven. The earthly sanctuary bore the same relationship to the old covenant as the heavenly sanctuary bears to the new covenant. The work carried on in the earthly sanctuary by the priests portrayed how God makes the covenant blessings available. Because Abraham's descendants broke the covenant they made with God, the ceremonies in the earthly sanctuary became necessary to save them from destruction.

All have broken their covenant with God, their pledge to render Him implicit obedience. Christ's mission in the heavenly sanctuary is necessary for anyone's salvation.

In both covenants, God the Father accepts the death of a substitute in place of man's destruction. In both, the obedience of a substitute replaces man's failure.

The old covenant pointed Israel to the new. The earthly

service had no value except as it developed faith in the heavenly. As faith in a substitute saved the repentant believer under the old covenant, so faith in their divine Substitute saves Christians today. Only as they bring to God an acceptable sacrifice can they find reconciliation with Him. That sacrifice is Christ.

The impressive service which depicted the purity and spotlessness of the sin bearer was a study in cleanliness and fastidiousness. Many have looked upon the Jewish era as a period of bloody ritual. They believed that the Tabernacle was a blood-stained building reeking with the remains of sacrificial animals. But such a picture of the Tabernacle designed by God is untrue. The Hebrew priests did everything with order and cleanliness. They carefully carried the remains of the sacrifices made in the court outside the camp for disposal. The blood not used in the service flowed away into the sand in the wilderness. The Temple in Jerusalem used a sewage system.

One must not assume that the beauty of the building itself was its most important part. Its significance lay in the service carried on inside. The Tabernacle with its priests, altars, and offerings existed for only one purpose—the process of atonement.

By presenting his sacrifice to the priest in the appointed manner, the sinner demonstrated his faith in the Redeemer to come. It revealed his total dependence in the "Lamb . . . which taketh away the sin of the world" as the only way of salvation.

The sanctuary system demonstrated how God severs men from their sins. The service justified the sinner before God and made him spiritually clean once more. Each day the symbolism of sacrificial blood transferred sins from the Israelite to the Tabernacle. As a result the sanctuary became defiled, for in it rested all the confessed sins of Israel until the Day of Atonement. Sin-free blood, rather than the sin-laden blood of the daily services, cleansed the Tabernacle on the Day of Atonement. The priest placed all the sins that had accumulated throughout the year on the scapegoat and had it led away into the desert—the land of forgetfulness.

As pointed out before, in patriarchal times the sinner confessed to the priest, who became the substitute, but, being a sinner himself, he could not represent the perfect sacrifice demanded by the law; so he killed the lamb as an atonement. The ceremony changed in the Levitical period. Instead of the priest killing the sacrifice, the sinner took the life of the animal with his own hand. The offering became the immediate substitute of the sinner, who directly confessed his transgression onto the animal in the presence of the priest. It thus became the sin bearer in type and had to die in the sinner's place.

The patriarchal service demonstrated through its types and symbols that Christ, man's High Priest, would assume his sins and then die in place of the guilty person. The Levitical service revealed how the Lamb of God—Christ—removes and destroys man's sins forever.

The two sets of ceremonies point out two vital truths— the death of the priest, and the death of the lamb. The types and ceremonies of both dispensations combine to reveal the significant fact that Jesus died as both Lamb and Priest. Truly, He was the complete Saviour, having been both the Offerer and Offering.

Seeing the need of a Saviour, a divine Substitute before the broken law, drove guilty Israel to the promises of the everlasting covenant illustrated in the sanctuary service. The Tabernacle services showed the sinner that God had provided an atonement between him and God the Father, that God would once again accept him.

Only in such a manner could Israel possibly keep the covenants they had entered into with God. The sanctuary service provided a system of mediatorial worship to meet God's requirements in their entirety, and it portrayed a substitute to satisfy the offended law while offering justice and mercy. The offerings of blood and incense daily reminded the people that only the merits of Christ, the true Mediator for Israel, could compensate for mankind's sin.

God did not create the sanctuary service for man to use as a means to earn merit and favor. Instead He devised the entire plan because it was painfully apparent that the Hebrews could not meet the claims of His law. Their efforts to obey it seemed only to plunge them into greater rebellion against God and into deep despair. Literal Israel found salvation just as spiritual Israel finds it today—through the merits of the divine Redeemer. Israel kept their covenant through a Mediator, just as the Christian church also keeps the new covenant through a Mediator.

While the law of God was the basis of the old covenant, an additional law formed a definite and integral part of the covenant—the ceremonial law, also given to Moses and designed by God. It governed the Hebrew sanctuary and stood at the center of the Jewish economy. But as the old covenant was temporary and provisional, so the ceremonial law was an ephemeral agreement to be discarded after the coming of the new dispensation.

Destined to regulate God's kingdom on earth and to portray Christ and His role through symbolism, the ceremonial law played its part. With the end of the Jewish nation, however, it no longer had any purpose. When Christ died on the cross, Israel, as a theocracy, a nation governed by God, ceased to exist, and with it went the ceremonial law. God fulfilled

His part of the old covenant. He had promised to be Israel's King, leading them to a territorial possession. As long as the Hebrews obeyed God's requirements, they controlled a specific geographical area. But when the murderous mob thundered, "We have no king but Caesar," the Jews gave up their chance to be a literal nation.

The ceremonial system consisted of symbols pointing to Christ, His sacrifice, and His priesthood. The Hebrews followed the ritual law with its sacrifices and ordinances until reality canceled the symbolism through Christ's death on the cross. Then all sacrificial offerings ceased. Then Christ "took it [the ceremonial law] out of the way, nailing it to his cross." (Colossians 2:14.)

"It is finished," Christ declared from the cross, and with the words ushered in another age. The service in the sanctuary in heaven was about to begin, for heaven's High Priest would soon arrive. Not by animal blood nor by ritualistic washings, incense, or ceremonies, but by His own death and perfect character, He would enter into the holy place. He had obtained eternal redemption for all who would accept Him as their Substitute.

# 11

# Atonement in the Court

AS POINTED OUT previously, the sanctuary service had two divisions, one daily, the other yearly. The priest performed services daily at the altar of burnt offering in the court, and in the holy place of the Tabernacle. The annual service took place in the most holy, the innermost, compartment and occurred on the Day of Atonement. The latter occasion ceremonially cleansed the sanctuary of the sins which had accumulated during the year.

The daily service consisted of the morning and evening burnt offering, the offering of sweet incense on the golden altar, and the special offerings for individual sins. In addition, the Hebrew religious system had offerings for Sabbaths, new moons, and special feasts.

The priests accomplished the atonement by the ceremonies held in all three areas of the Tabernacle. Each act in this symbolic portrayal of Christ depended upon the proceedings in the other parts of the sanctuary.

The court occupied a peculiar place in the Tabernacle because all services had their beginnings there. There the Hebrews made ready for the important proceedings to be conducted in the Tabernacle. There the sacrifice took place. There the priest burned each morning and evening a year-old lamb upon the altar. The two primary factors of the atonement ceremony, the shed blood of animals and the smoke of burning incense, originated in the courtyard.

The Apostle Paul described the two apartments of the Tabernacle on earth as being "figures of the true." (Hebrews 9:24.) God showed Moses the sanctuary in heaven and told him to pattern the earthly one after it. (Hebrews 8:5; 9:23.) John the revelator, taken in vision to heaven, saw the heavenly prototype. God revealed to Daniel, Ezekiel, and David an understanding of the celestial sanctuary. All would agree that the earthly sanctuary was an elaborate visual aid to daily teach the people about the atonement of the heavenly sanctuary and to point them to Christ.

Considering the court of the heavenly sanctuary, the Bible student finds clear evidence as to its existence and location:

1. The earthly, or typical, sanctuary had a court.

2. The Bible supports its presence.

In Revelation 11:1, 2 the Apostle John states, "And there was given me a reed like unto a rod: and the angel stood, saying, Rise, and measure the temple of God, and the altar, and them that worship therein. But the court which is without the temple leave out, and measure it not; for it is given unto the Gentiles: and the holy city shall they tread under foot forty and two months."

The passage makes a definite reference to the heavenly sanctuary, including the altar in the court, for when John wrote the Book of Revelation, the Temple lay in ruins, destroyed by the Romans.

The angel told John not to measure the court since the Gentiles would possess it for a definite period of time. The forty and two months mentioned is a reiteration of the 1260-year prophecy of Daniel 7:25. The court here represents the earth. No other part of the heavenly sanctuary could be given to the Gentiles, because the first and second apartments are in heaven. Also the court is where the priest slew the victims whose blood he would minister in the sanctuary. To fulfill the symbolism of the earthly sanctuary, the victim in the heavenly sanctuary must die in the court—and Christ died on Calvary in Judaea.

"We have an altar, whereof they have no right to eat which serve the tabernacle." Hebrews 13:10. This verse helps in identifying the court. Christians have an altar—the cross of Calvary—and a sacrifice far surpassing the ancient animal sacrifices in value. Since the cross is the altar of the Christian, following through the symbolism, the court must be the earth, for the Hebrews located the altar in the court.

The altar in the typical service represents the cross on which Christ died. He offered Himself as the supreme sacrificial victim in a courtyard that comprises an entire planet. The Christian now stands in the outer court, waiting for his divine High Priest to come from the inner courts of heaven and bring a close to the antitypical Day of Atonement.

With this conception of the earth being the court of the heavenly sanctuary, Christ's part in the atonement becomes clearer. Like the priest in the typical service, Jesus, the Christian's Priest, was born to His position. "Lo, I come (in the volume of the book it is written of me,) to do thy will, O God." Hebrews 10:7. Unlike the human priest, Christ had accepted His role before His birth among men. Parts of the fifth and sixth verses of the fifth chapter of Hebrews stress Christ's prebirth acceptance: "Thou art my Son, to day have I begotten thee. . . . Thou art a priest for ever after the order of Melchisedec."

The question arises in the mind of the Bible student as to what Jesus did during the thirty obscure years He spent in the carpenter's shop. Why was it necessary for Him to endure this period of poverty before He embarked upon His public ministry? What did it have to do with the atonement?

When one considers the fact that all the redeemed must present a perfect human life before God when He judges all men, the answer becomes obvious. Only the Sinless One could see that man passes the judgment. He alone fully lived out the principles of the law as man's Substitute and Surety. He alone developed a perfect human character, not just for Himself but for every repentant sinner.

The Hebrew priesthood sacrificed the lamb in the court. Christ was the symbolic Lamb. John the Baptist cried of Him, "Behold the Lamb of God, which taketh away the sin of the world." John 1:29.

Christ's mediatorial position depended upon the phase of His priesthood which He developed in the court. Without the preparatory service, no atonement could be made. Christ had to live His life on earth as a man among men.

# 12

# The Incense

SINCE the fall of man, the world has had no direct communication with God the Father. Its only connection has been through Jesus Christ.

This relationship was demonstrated in the twenty-five-century-long patriarchal dispensation. The sanctuary system given to Moses, a more elaborate plan, existed for another fifteen hundred years, a period called the Aaronic or legal dispensation. Both services carried on in types and symbols the process of atonement, prefiguring the coming Saviour, the Priest of the gospel dispensation.

Never did a priest enter the Tabernacle without the two vital symbols of blood and incense. These symbols were necessary to the process of atonement, and they pointed forward to the real means of atonement.

Obviously the blood of the typical service pointed to the death of Christ. Innumerable Biblical references attest to this fact. Many passages in the Old Testament point forward to the death of Christ. In the New Testament, the Gospel writers reiterate specifically that the blood in the Hebrew sanctuary services typified Christ's blood. Jesus Himself stated that His blood was the true sacrifice and that no man could approach God except through Him.

As for the other factor, the incense, one finds the word used often in the Bible, usually in the context of the earthly Tabernacle. The Greek verb *thumiaō* (to burn incense), or the noun *thumiama* (incense) appears seven times in the New Testament. Only three instances pertain to the incense of the sanctuary in heaven. The latter passages occur in the Book of Revelation, which pictures the divine Priest as He ministers in the celestial apartments.

"And another angel came and stood at the altar, having a golden censer; and there was given unto him much incense, that he should offer it *with* the prayers of all saints upon the golden altar which was before the throne. And the smoke of the incense, which came *with* the prayers of the saints, ascended up before God out of the angel's hand." Revelation 8:3, 4.

The use of the preposition "with" rules out the possibility that the incense is the prayers of the saints. Instead, the passage indicates that the angel offers the incense along with the saints' prayers. An earlier verse does compare prayer to fragrant odors, though: "And when he had taken the book, the four beasts and four and twenty elders fell down before the Lamb, having every one of them harps, and golden vials full of odours, which are the prayers of the saints." Revelation 5:8.

The incense, ascending with the prayers of Israel, it would seem, represented the merits and the intercession of Christ, including His perfect character. Before the veil of the most holy place stood an altar of perpetual intercession, and before the holy place, one of continual atonement. The priests approached God through the symbols of blood and incense. Both the priest and the symbols of blood and incense point to the work of Christ, the great Mediator, who makes salvation possible to those willing to accept it.

At the morning and evening services, the priests offered daily sacrifice upon the altar in the court outside, and their petitions ascended with the cloud of incense. The Christian believer confesses his sins, and Christ's righteousness mingles with his repentance, that the prayer of the fallen may rise like fragrant incense before the Father. In Isaiah 27:5 Christ says through the prophet, "Let him take hold of my strength, that he may make peace with me; and he shall make peace with me."

With the conception of the incense representing the merits of Christ, a clearer picture of the atonement develops. Having lived a perfect and sinless life as the second Adam, not for Himself but for every repentant sinner, He stands as man's Substitute before God. His death was a necessity in God's plan, but what would it have meant had He not lived a perfect life?

Christ's death reconciles man to God because it paid the penalty for sin. However, someone must demonstrate a perfect sinless life and character in order for an individual to gain entrance into heaven. The saved must be declared sinless in Christ—as if they had never sinned—thus appearing without fault before the holy law. Only the attributes of Christ can meet such a standard. He presents His character and life in place of the repentant sinner's on judgment day. Faulty though our lives may have been, through the wonders of the atonement God writes pardon opposite our names.

Through the atoning blood of Christ, the sinner is set free from guilt and sin. Without Christ he would have to remain a sinner forever. Faith in Christ makes man just before God. It is the only way the fallen race can approach the Father and be assured of acceptance and complete deliverance from sin.

The garment of acceptance which all the redeemed will wear is woven without a thread of human endeavor. Such is the incense of the antitypical service. It is His righteous character.

Thus in the sanctuary services we see that God is to be approached only by the blood and incense of Christ.

# 13

# The Day of Atonement

THE HOLY OF HOLIES, or innermost compartment, of the sanctuary on earth served as the connecting link between heaven and earth. No mortal eye saw the chamber beyond the inner veil except the high priest on the Day of Atonement. For any other person to enter at any time meant instant death.

Like the first apartment, its walls were overlaid with pure gold. In the center of the room stood the sole piece of furniture—the ark of the covenant. Made of acacia wood, it also had an overlay of gold outside and in. A glittering crown of gold bordered the cover, which was called the mercy seat. The magnificent chest contained the two tables of stone upon which God had recorded His sacred law. The ark represented the throne of God in heaven.

The mercy seat consisted of one solid piece of gold. On each end stood a cherub also of pure gold, one wing folded over the body while the other stretched upward. In Solomon's Temple, two other golden angels, larger in size, stood at each end on the floor, their faces looking reverently down on the sacred ark. These symbolized the heavenly angels who stand by the throne of God, guarding the sacred law.

Between the cherubim appeared the visible manifestation of the divine presence, the glorious Shekinah. From here God made known His will to the high priest, at times communicating with him audibly. And from it—through the Atonement —God granted pardon from eternal death. With great fear and trembling the human mediator prepared himself to lift the veil and enter into the actual presence of Deity.

Trumpets blowing on the first day of the seventh month warned Israel that the great Day of Atonement would soon arrive. The most solemn ceremony of the year must find them well prepared. They had looked forward to the sacred service in eager, but solemn, anticipation. Finally, the tenth day of the month arrived.

The high priest would perform the ceremony removing the sins which had previously been transferred to the sanctuary. The year-long process of atonement reached its climax with the cancellation of all confessed transgression. The "defiled" sanctuary had to be "cleansed" from the "uncleanness" of the children of Israel through the ritual described in Leviticus 16:19. All who came up to the day unprepared would be "cut off" from the congregation forever.

As the high priest prepared for the ceremony, the people gathered around the Tabernacle in mourning and humiliation. First he removed his colorful pontifical robes, for, like the lesser priests who ministered in the daily service, he would officiate in a plain white linen garment.

The high priest's clothing had deep symbolism. God Himself had designated the material, colors, and style of the robes. While the common priests wore a simple garment of spotless white linen, God commanded the high priest to wear in addition an attire made up of pleasing shades of blue, purple, scarlet, and gold, decorated with many precious stones. A miter bearing a plate of gold engraved with the words "Holiness to the Lord" rested upon his head. An elaborately embroidered and jeweled breastplate set with twelve gem stones bore the names of the twelve tribes of Israel over the priest's heart.

It was important that everything worn by the priests be whole and without blemish, for the garments represented the character of Jesus Christ.

The high priest depicted Christ, who would become a high priest after the manner of Melchizedek, an order of priesthood that would not pass to another or be superseded by someone else.

Though Christ *serves* like the Levitical priests, He was *called* in the same way as the great priest-king of the patriarchal dispensation. No other human priest so closely typified Christ's role as did the mysterious Melchizedek. As there was only one Melchizedek, so there is only one Christ.

The robe of the common priests who conducted the daily sacrificial service symbolized the spotless character of the incarnate Christ. The magnificent pontifical robes of the high priest who ministered in the yearly service hinted at the unspeakable majesty of the Saviour's deity.

Aaron held the position of counselor and judge, and next to Moses he was the highest authority in the nation. His impressive attire made his presence commanding and imposing. His authority and power in many ways ranked with that of the voice of God to the people, and there was no appeal from his decisions. On the Jewish day of final atonement, he alone could officiate.

The people who assembled around the sanctuary learned something of the great sacrifice that the Messiah would make in their behalf. As they saw Aaron emerge from the sanctuary, stripped of his usual magnificent apparel, they had an opportunity to sense how Christ would lay aside His splendor and glory and come to earth, not as a King, but as a servant in the garb of fallen humanity.

The people fasted and prayed during the Day of Atonement. One question occupied their thoughts: Would the high priest bearing their sins find acceptance with God?

In his simple linen garment, Aaron went into the courtyard where a young bullock waited to be offered. He confessed no sin on the victim. It would make atonement for Aaron himself and "his house," the Levitical priesthood. As the people's representatives, the priests legally fell under the sentence of death for the vicarious sins they bore. At one time Moses said to Aaron's sons, "God hath given it you to bear the iniquity of the congregation." Leviticus 10:17.

As the bullock was slain, the people watched its dying agonies. In the death of the innocent beast, they saw the death of Jesus.

One phase of Jesus' Priesthood was that of dying on the cross. He died as Priest for His people, having taken upon Himself the world's sins, assuming all of mankind's guilt. It was not physical agony which brought about His death. Christ died from a broken heart, from such mental anguish as man shall never know.

As the high priest performed the ceremony of death, doubtless his robe, at first spotlessly white, became spattered with the blood of the animal. And as the spotless robe of the priest became stained, the people recalled their failures and shortcomings during the past year. Each person realized the hopelessness of his condition without the work of the mediator.

With a vessel containing the animal's blood in one hand and a golden censer filled with sacred incense in the other, Aaron solemnly entered the sanctuary, passing into the holy of holies. There in the presence of God he sprinkled the mercy seat above the law with blood seven times. The number seven signified a perfect sacrifice. The cloud of incense which filled the apartment stood for the sinless life which Jesus lived as the sinner's Substitute. Thus a complete atonement was made for the sinner—no conflict remained between God's justice and His mercy. He could maintain the authority of His law and still extend pardon to the penitent sinner.

Next the priest left the most holy place and sprinkled the blood seven times on the golden altar of incense in the first apartment, which had been "defiled" by the sin-laden blood during the daily services. Then he went out into the courtyard and cleansed the altar of burnt offering in the same manner. The remains of the sacrificial animal were then removed from the premises and burned.

The priest had made an atonement for himself and the rest of the priesthood. Now he completed the service of reconciliation for the people.

The people brought forward two goats, and Aaron cast lots upon them, thereby choosing one to represent the Saviour and one to stand for the originator of sin. Satan must bear the final punishment for all the sins he has caused the righteous to commit. The great enemy of man must be punished for the sins which caused the Saviour to suffer such agony.

As the high priest took the life of the "Lord's goat," his robe became even more spotted with blood. This was the day of judgment. It was now too late to become reconciled to God. After the judgment the unrepentant must bear their own iniquity.

The high priest took the blood of the innocent kid along with incense into the inner sanctuary and followed the same ritual he had performed with the bullock's blood. The removal of the goat's body to be burned outside the encampment symbolized that Jesus would die outside the gates of Jerusalem for the sins of the world. Both sacrifices, that of the bullock and that of the goat, symbolized the death of Christ. Perhaps the bullock's sacrifice showed Christ's death as Priest and the offering of the goat indicated His death as Victim.

Upon departing from the sanctuary, the priest in his role of mediator took upon himself all the confessed sins of the people. In the courtyard he laid his hands on the head of the scapegoat and transferred the transgressions symbolically to the goat Azazel. A "fit man" led it far into the wilderness, where it could never return to camp. Not until then did the people consider themselves finally free from the past year's sins. The atonement was now completed. The high priest returned to the first apartment, removed his stained linen robe, bathed, put on a clean white garment, and over it, his elaborate pontifical robes. After this deeply significant act, he came out and blessed the waiting people.

The prophet Daniel plainly foretold the time when the last work of atonement would take place. (See chapter 24.) He spoke of the last cleansing of the sanctuary in heaven, when the record of sin would be removed from the dwelling place of God. Heaven has kept a faithful account of each man's life. Those who have accepted Jesus as their Saviour have pardon registered by their names, and they follow their Priest by faith into the audience chamber of God.

Just as the sanctuary on earth was a copy of the sanctuary in heaven, so what was in the earthly also exists in the heavenly. Just as the service on earth revolved around the broken law written on two tables of stone, so the service in heaven centers around the original transcript of the same law. As there are two sanctuaries, two covenants, two priesthoods, so there have been two transcripts of the law, one on earth, the other in heaven.

The law given on Sinai declared the principle of love. It was a revelation to the earth of the law of heaven. The

Being who spoke it possessed the power to bring men's hearts into harmony with its principles. God revealed the purpose of the law when He said to Israel, "Ye shall be holy men unto me." Exodus 22:31.

The law had no power to pardon the transgressor. Christ as Mediator came between God and man *to unite man with God by bringing him into allegiance to His law*. Jesus alone could pay the debt of the sinner, *but the fact that He has paid does not give the transgressor the freedom to continue to disobey God's law*.

Before the sacred law of God Heaven weighs men's characters. Every thought, deed, emotion, or motive is examined as carefully as though the person involved were the only sinner to be brought before heaven's tribunal. Judged by the constitution of the universe, all men find themselves hopelessly condemned. Not a single act of their lives can bear the scrutiny of the great Detector of sin, for imperfect human nature has corrupted even their most noble deeds.

Jesus is in the most holy place of the heavenly sanctuary completing the final work of atonement for man. The investigative judgment is now accepting or rejecting each person as a future inhabitant of heaven. No one knows when his life will come up for review. But for those who have accepted Christ as their Saviour, the Redeemer will step forward as their Priest and Advocate. He will present His death and perfect life and request heaven's court not to judge the sinner's imperfect life, but His perfect one. Christ's sin-laden blood bore the transgressions of the believer to the sanctuary. His sin-free blood will blot out the sins, while the incense of His righteousness will make the believer fit for heaven. God looks not at the sinner, but at his Substitute. The mandate will go forth, "He that is righteous, let him be righteous still."

Revelation 22:11. The man who puts his faith in Jesus as his Redeemer will have his sins transferred to the account of Satan, and heaven's records will be closed. No one will ever again register a charge of transgression against his name.

"Blessed is he whose transgression is forgiven, whose sin is covered," the Bible declares. "Blessed is the man unto whom the Lord imputeth not iniquity, and in whose spirit there is no guile." "I acknowledged my sin unto thee, and mine iniquity have I not hid. I said, I will confess my transgressions unto the Lord; and thou forgavest the iniquity of my sin." Psalm 32:1, 2, 5.

"Repent ye therefore, and be converted, that your sins may be blotted out, when the times of refreshing shall come from the presence of the Lord." Acts 3:19.

The person who has the perfect Substitute to take his place before that law knows that the Father will be reconciled to him when his name is called in the judgment. He will find the great Lawgiver a merciful and compassionate Father, who will welcome the prodigal home with open arms and place about him His own beautiful robe, which is without stain.

While investigation goes on, Jesus still offers His blood in the sinner's behalf. The incense of His righteousness still ascends with the Christian's prayers. His merits, self-denial, and self-sacrifice Heaven treasures as incense to be offered with the prayers of His people. As the sinner's prayers—sincere and humble—reach the throne of God, Christ mingles with them the merits of His own life of perfect obedience.

When the priest in the days of Israel explained these truths to the waiting congregation, they felt deep gratitude that God had provided such a plan. The people knew that a day would come when God would erase their records of sin, not only in type, but in reality.

# 14

# The Passover

THE TWELFTH CHAPTER of Exodus describes graphically the origin of the Jewish Passover service, a ceremony with an important relationship to mankind's atonement. "In the tenth day of this month they shall take to them every man a lamb, according to the house of their fathers, a lamb for an house: and if the household be too little for the lamb, let him and his neighbour next unto his house take it according to the number of the souls; every man according to his eating shall make your count for the lamb.

"Your lamb shall be without blemish, a male of the first year: ye shall take it out from the sheep, or from the goats: and ye shall keep it up until the fourteenth day of the same month: and the whole assembly of the congregation of Israel shall kill it in the evening. And they shall take of the blood, and strike it on the two side posts and on the upper door post of the houses, wherein they shall eat it.

"And they shall eat the flesh in that night, roast with fire, and unleavened bread; and with bitter herbs they shall eat it. Eat not of it raw, nor sodden at all with water, but roast with fire; his head with his legs, and with the purtenance thereof. And ye shall let nothing of it remain until the morning; and that which remaineth of it until the morning ye shall burn with fire.

"And thus shall ye eat it; with your loins girded, your shoes on your feet, and your staff in your hand; and ye shall eat it in haste: it is the Lord's passover. For I will pass through the land of Egypt this night, and will smite all the firstborn in the land of Egypt, both man and beast; and against all the gods of Egypt I will execute judgment: I am the Lord.

"And the blood shall be to you for a token upon the houses where ye are: and when I see the blood, I will pass over you, and the plague shall not be upon you to destroy you, when I smite the land of Egypt.

"And this day shall be unto you for a memorial; and ye shall keep it a feast to the Lord throughout your generations; ye shall keep it a feast by an ordinance for ever. Seven days shall ye eat unleavened bread; even the first day ye shall put away leaven out of your houses: for whosoever eateth leavened bread from the first day until the seventh day, that soul shall be cut off from Israel.

"And in the first day there shall be an holy convocation, and in the seventh day there shall be an holy convocation to you; no manner of work shall be done in them, save that which every man must eat, that only may be done of you.

"And ye shall observe the feast of unleavened bread; for in this selfsame day have I brought your armies out of the land of Egypt: therefore shall ye observe this day in your generations by an ordinance for ever." Verses 3-17.

Some 3,500 years ago, according to the Scriptures, a new nation came into being. With its beginning occurred the first Passover, when God freed Israel from Egyptian slavery—on the "selfsame day" (Exodus 12:41) as predicted in the vision given to Abraham (Genesis 15:13). Centuries of servitude had reduced the Israelites to an illiterate mass of rabble. History reveals no more spectacular event than the manner in which God elected to free His people, for He had chosen them to demonstrate to the world and to celestial beings what He could do with humanity dedicated to Him.

The negotiations of Moses with Pharaoh and the plagues that devastated Egypt because of her refusal to liberate Israel are familiar historical facts. Passover day derives its name from the climactic event of the day, the slaying of every first-born man and beast in the land on the fourteenth. At midnight the Passover angel "passed over" Egypt, smiting all the first-born unprotected by the blood of the paschal lamb. "In the fourteenth day of the first month at even is the Lord's pass-over." Leviticus 23:5. The prophetic types saw their fulfill-ment not only in the event, but as to time. Christ, the Passover Lamb, was slain on the same day and month that type had marked out fifteen long centuries before.

After describing and identifying the date of Passover day, Moses in Exodus 12:6 reveals the ritualistic ordinance the people should follow. He states of the lamb, "And ye shall keep it up until the fourteenth day of the same month: and the whole assembly of the congregation of Israel shall kill it in the evening."

To be preserved, then, they had to sacrifice the animal "at even, at the going down of the sun." (Deuteronomy 16:6.) Apparently they killed it and sprinkled its blood on the lintel sometime before midnight to satisfy the Passover covenant and to protect the firstborn.

Unlike other feast days, Passover day was a home service. The people observed and carried out its ritual during the first part of the night. The significance of "this night" assumes great proportions, for the events of Israel's freedom occurred during Passover night. "I will pass through the land of Egypt this night." Exodus 12:12. "And they shall eat the flesh in that night." Verse 8. "At midnight the Lord smote all the firstborn in the land of Egypt." Verse 29. "And he called for Moses and Aaron by night, and said, Rise up, and get you forth from among my people . . . and go." Verse 31. "It is a night to be much observed unto the Lord for bringing them out from the land of Egypt: this is that night of the Lord to be observed of all the children of Israel in their generations." Verse 42. "And it came to pass, that at midnight the Lord smote all the firstborn in the land of Egypt, from the firstborn of Pharaoh that sat on his throne unto the firstborn of the captive that was in the dungeon; and all the firstborn of cattle." Verse 29.

Inspired history records how Pharaoh, under the stimulation of the last and most terrible of the plagues, hastily granted Israel its liberty after the Passover angel had come at midnight. (Exodus 12:30, 31.)

Down through the ages Israel has observed Passover day, the fourteenth of Abib, as their independence day, their Fourth of July. It commemorated their emancipation from Egypt. In addition it pointed forward to Christ's deliverance of His people from the bondage of sin.

On the first Passover night God commanded the Jews, "None of you shall go out at the door of his house until the morning." Exodus 12:22. Hastily the Israelites, over one million strong, prepared to leave. After so many years of slavery, they were comparable to the American slaves at the time of the Civil War, being uneducated and superstitious. In addition, a "mixed multitude," apparently composed of Egyptian believers and others, went with them. Perhaps the exodus consisted of two million people on foot with their possessions and herds.

Before they left, the Israelites obtained funds for their journey from their captors. "They borrowed of the Egyptians jewels of silver, and jewels of gold, and raiment: and the Lord gave the people favour in the sight of the Egyptians, so that they lent unto them such things as they required. And they spoiled the Egyptians." Exodus 12:35, 36.

With so large a gathering, it seems difficult that they could leave on such short notice. But apparently they had made some secret plans for the departure, for the Bible states, "And they departed from Rameses in the first month, on the fifteenth day of the first month; on the morrow after the passover the children of Israel went out with an high hand in the sight of all the Egyptians." Numbers 33:3.

Only one record of their observing Passover on the wilderness journey exists. (Numbers 9:1-5.) Moses did, however, instruct them to keep it in the "promised land." (Exodus 12:25.)

The seven-day Feast of Unleavened Bread immediately followed Passover day. "In the fourteenth day of the first month at even is the Lord's passover. And on the fifteenth day of the same month is the feast of unleavened bread unto the Lord: seven days ye must eat unleavened bread." Leviticus 23: 5, 6. A joyous occasion, it commemorated liberation from Egypt and looked forward to freedom from sin for all of God's people.

The happy celebration began on the fifteenth with a sabbath and lasted seven days, through the twenty-first, also a ceremonial sabbath. The book *Patriarchs and Prophets*, by Ellen G. White, page 539, describes the occasion: "The Passover was followed by the seven days' feast of unleavened bread. The first and the seventh day were days of holy convocation, when no servile work was to be performed. On the second day of the feast, the first-fruits of the year's harvest were presented before God. Barley was the earliest grain in Palestine, and at the opening of the feast it was beginning to ripen. A sheaf of this grain was waved by the priest before

107

the altar of God, as an acknowledgment that all was His. Not until this ceremony had been performed was the harvest to be gathered."

So while Passover day was a mournful occasion, observed by the sacrifice of a life through death, resulting in deliverance and freedom, the festival which came after it was a time of happiness. The scene also changed from the home back to the Temple with its daily sacrifices of the morning and evening lambs. The fifteenth saw special offerings consisting of two young bullocks, one ram, seven lambs of the first year, and one goat. (Numbers 28:19-23.) The offering of the "wave sheaf" took place on the sixteenth, and further pageantry continued throughout the remainder of the week.

Much of the significance of the Passover lies in the fact that it is perhaps the strongest type in the Bible relating to Christ as Saviour. Paul correctly said, "Christ our passover is sacrificed for us." 1 Corinthians 5:7. For 1,500 years, the Jewish nation celebrated the day that Christ would die, yet they failed to recognize Him as their Messiah.

God used the Passover season to focus worldwide attention on His Son. Palestine, being situated in Asia Minor, stood at the crossroads of the then-known world. It was located between Europe, Asia, and Africa, on routes used by travelers to the teeming continents. In addition, the Passover was one of the three feast days of Israel. Thousands came to take part in the holy service.

The startling news of Jesus' unjust trial, persecution, and crucifixion spread by word of mouth to all nations with a minimum of delay. Many of the visitors in Palestine were men of influence, representatives from foreign courts, kings, noblemen, princes. They witnessed the death of Christ, and the events deeply troubled them. Returning home, filled with awe, they related all that they had seen and heard.

Christ wanted the death of His beloved Son to be the great center of attraction, both then and now.

Christ followed the type in all details pertaining to Him. In the Passover service, the Jews selected the lamb on the tenth day of the month of Abib and set it aside, never to be changed for another.

Similarly, Christ's triumphal entry into Jerusalem occurred on the tenth day of Abib when He accepted for the first time the people's homage as their King. The procession assembled outside the Holy City on Sunday, the first day of the week, and the ninth day of Abib. But Christ waited until the setting sun before He rode into Jerusalem. As all days began at sundown under the Jewish calendar, so the tenth began then when God the Son voluntarily set Himself aside as the antitypical Passover Lamb. Jesus knew that once He entered the city, He could not change His course. The path led through the sheepgate, where the sacrificial animals were brought in, and from there to the altar (the cross), where mankind would slay the Lamb of the world.

From the age of twelve, Jesus understood that He was the antitype of the paschal lamb. It was then that He witnessed the sacred ceremony for the first time. As He looked on with intense interest, the Holy Spirit revealed to Him the purpose of the service. Every act of the white-robed priest and the bleeding victim seemed to be firmly bound up with His own life. New impulses awakened within Him. The mystery of His mission began to open to the Saviour.

The Passover observance held a mournful attraction to the Son of God. He saw in the slain lamb the symbol of His death, and He watched with a certain fascination as the priests instructed the congregation celebrating this ordinance.

The Saviour lived a life of obedience to the Jewish law, and the Passover was no exception. Before His crucifixion the disciples came to Christ and asked where they would observe the Passover. (Matthew 26:17; Mark 14:12; Luke 22:7-9.) The previous Passovers they had celebrated together had been scenes of special interest, but this time something greatly troubled Jesus. He knew that the day had come when He must die as a sacrifice for the sin of the world. As the Antitype of the paschal lamb, He understood that men would kill Him on the day the Jews would eat the Passover.

The Passover type saw its fulfillment exactly as foretold centuries before. The Passover ordinances had designated the month and the day. (Numbers 28:16.) God's timetable had arrived at the time when type would meet antitype. Christ now stood in the shadow of the cross.

Ellen G. White comments, "These types were fulfilled, not only as to the event, but as to the time. On the fourteenth day of the first Jewish month, the very day and month on which for fifteen long centuries the Passover lamb had been slain, Christ, having eaten the Passover with His disciples, instituted that feast which was to commemorate His own death as 'the Lamb of God, which taketh away the sin of the world.' That same night He was taken by wicked hands to be crucified and slain. And as the antitype of the wave sheaf, our Lord was raised from the dead on the third day, 'the first fruits of them that slept,' a sample of all the resurrected just, whose 'vile body' shall be changed, and 'fashioned like unto His glorious body.'"—*The Great Controversy*, p. 399.

Christ's death is the climax of the atonement, the central theme around which all other events cluster. As such it is the greatest and most magnificent type in the Bible, fixed from eternity as to the year, the month, the day, and the hour. Down through the ages men have attempted to discredit God's Word, but it vindicates itself. The prophet Daniel predicted the last Passover supper in his 2300-day prophecy (Daniel 8:14; 9:24-27), and the Passover ordinances described in Exodus set the month and day. The evening sacrifice had foretold the hour when Christ would utter His last words, "It is finished." The morning daily lamb indicated the time the Romans placed Jesus on the cross.

Ever true to sacred type, Jesus died on Passover day. As a memorial to the Sabbath, He rested in the grave on the fifteenth, which was both a ceremonial and weekly Sabbath that year. Then to give hope to those who through the years have died trusting in Him as their Saviour, He arose on wave sheaf day, the sixteenth, as the firstfruits of salvation.

When Christ celebrated the last Passover with His disciples, type began to meet antitype. Men no longer had a need to slay the paschal lamb "at even" on the fourteenth day of Abib. No longer do God's followers need to show obedience to His command to eat of the bitter herbs and unleavened bread. Our Lord fulfilled them.

As a result, the era of type vanished. The believer now has the privilege of coming boldly into the audience chamber of the Most High, bearing the merits of Christ, his Passover. No longer do we observe the day, but its events take on added importance to us as we contemplate the wonders of the atonement the Passover so vividly demonstrated. We rejoice that the blood Christ shed enables us to stand perfect in Him before the God of the universe.

Only in the light of the atonement does the Passover assume its full significance. Under the terms of the everlasting covenant, Christ promised to make an atonement for fallen humanity, a covenant renewed to Adam, Noah, Abraham,

111

Isaac, and the nation of Israel. When "Christ our passover . . . [was] sacrificed for us" at Calvary on Passover day, His death ratified the holy covenant of peace. Thus all the types and prophecies of the old covenant dispensation relative to the Saviour's sacrifice saw their completion on "the selfsame day," the fourteenth of Abib.

# 15

# The Passover Type Fulfilled

FOR MANY CENTURIES the Hebrew people had witnessed the Passover, each generation carrying on the rituals taught them by those who had preceded them. Now the sun was setting and marking the close of the thirteenth day of Nisan (formerly called Abib), A.D. 31, and again all of Jerusalem was preparing to celebrate the Passover. A day was ending and a new one beginning "at even."

This year the fourteenth came on a Friday. The Passover lamb would then be slain according to the commandment. Around the time of the Passover the holy city became a scene of muffled excitement. Eight days of ceremony would begin at sunset marking the close of Thursday. Pilgrims from far and near assembled to take part in the Passover festivities, the most widely attended of all Israel's feasts.

The rumors about the Sanhedrin's plot to put to death Jesus, who claimed to be the Son of God, put tension into the night air. As all faithful Israelites did, the Saviour and His disciples assembled in a prearranged upper room to take part in the Passover supper. But the disciples did not seem to sense the significance of this day. The New Testament writers, however, did afterward recognize its importance, for the Four Gospels alone devote a total of 535 verses to this antitypical Passover day.

The climax of the sacrificial atonement would occur before the sun set again. The stroke of death at about the "ninth hour," or three o'clock in the afternoon, would complete the transition from the Levitical to the gospel dispensation.

The Passover season began while the moon was full. Each month in the ancient Jewish calendar was a lunar one because the Hebrews reckoned it from one visible new moon to the next. Hence Nisan 14 would coincide with the time of full moon. Furthermore, Nisan 16—the day after the annual sabbath (Nisan 15)—was the date on which the Jews would wave a sheaf of the ripening new crop of barley, the earliest grain harvested during the year in Palestine, as an offering of firstfruits to the Lord. The people could not harvest the grain until the priests had performed the sacred rite. Because of the synchronization of the paschal season with the barley harvest in Bible times, the Jews always kept the Passover in the springtime, a time of the year when daylight and darkness were almost equal in length.

Coming to the upper room at "even" (about six o'clock), Christ remained for approximately three hours. Afterward, as was His custom, He retired to the Garden of Gethsemane to pray. He knew full well the blood-stained path upon which His feet had entered. Soon His hour would come when He must suffer and die as the transgressor of the holy law. His disciples went with Him to His favored retreat, while the Passover moon, broad and full, shone down upon them from a cloudless sky. Slowly they made their way deeper into the recesses of the Garden, the city of pilgrims' tents now hushed into silence.

Jesus asked all but three of His disciples to remain in a secluded place, taking with Him Peter, James, and John. Coming upon His usual place of privacy, He felt strange and mysterious stirrings of guilt engulfing Him. Every step became one of labored effort. His companions studied Him, puzzled,

114

for they had never seen Him in such mental distress. He appeared to suffer under the pressure of a terrible burden. They reached out, supporting Him to prevent Him from falling. His body convulsed with anguish, and His pale countenance expressed a sorrow beyond description.

The New Testament records that He went a short distance from the three of them and fell prostrate upon the ground. He felt Himself being separated from His Father by a gulf of sin so broad and black and deep that His spirit shuddered before it.

Innocent though Christ was, Heaven accounted Him guilty, and the punishment of the broken law gripped Him. Through trembling lips He cried out, "O my Father, if it be possible, let this cup pass from me: nevertheless not as I will, but as thou wilt." Matthew 26:39. He experienced what every sinner will feel who does not have a Mediator to stand between him and God. As He felt the separation developing between Himself and the Father, He feared that His humanity would falter and fail in the coming conflict with the prince of darkness. The sins of the world weighed heavily upon the Saviour, bowing Him to the earth.

The destiny of the human race had been at stake during His earlier conflict with Satan in the wilderness, but Christ had then conquered. Now the tempter entered the Garden for the last fearful struggle with Jesus. Satan had prepared for the encounter during the three years of Christ's ministry. If he failed, his hope of controlling the earth was lost.

The disciples had experienced a long and wearying day. They were extremely tired, and despite the troubling scene of the Saviour's anguish, they soon fell asleep, leaving Him alone in His suffering.

At the end of an hour (Mark 14:37), Jesus felt the need

115

for human sympathy. With painful effort He returned to the place where He had left His companions, only to find them asleep.

Again superhuman agony seized Him, and He staggered back, faint and exhausted, to the scene of His former struggle. Alone, He fell prostrate to the ground, with only the cypress and the palms as silent witnesses. After another period of fervent prayer to His Father, He returned to again find the three deep in sleep. His presence awakened them, but He did not speak to them, as He had on the previous occasion. His blood-stained face filled the disciples with fear. They could not account for the turmoil of mind expressed in their Saviour's face.

Sadly He returned to His retreat, a sense of the sins of the world almost overwhelming Him. The moment of decision had come. The destiny of the world trembled in the balance. But even then the Majesty of heaven could have wiped the bloody sweat from the brow of His Son, leaving men to reap the results of their iniquity. Would the innocent Christ willingly suffer the consequence of God's wrath to save guilty man?

Again He implored His heavenly Father, "O my Father, if this cup may not pass away from me, except I drink it, thy will be done." Matthew 26:42.

Alone in the Garden He endured the sinner's sense of guilt, condemned before the holy law. Three times His humanity shrank from the last crowning sacrifice. Three times He prayed to His Father. But then He realized that the transgressor, if left to himself, must perish under the displeasure of the heavenly Father. He recognized the power of sin over men, and the utter inability of man to save himself.

At last He made His decision. He would save man at

whatever cost to Himself. Having left the courts of heaven to save the one world that had fallen by transgression, He would not turn back from the mission He had chosen.

No human friend supported Him in His hour of need, but God suffered with Him. It was the greatest evidence of His Father's love to mankind that the Infinite Father would send His Son to earth to endure poverty, contempt, agony, and death for the rebellious human race.

But to sustain the Lord under His terrible burden, Heaven sent a messenger to minister to Him. The radiance of the celestial being who supported the head of their Master suddenly aroused the disciples from their slumber. The angel had come to let Christ know that while the cup was not to be taken from Him, He would be supported in drinking it. Upon the face of the Saviour now rested a deep serenity.

For a third time the disciples awakened. "Sleep on now, and take your rest," Christ said. "Behold, the hour is at hand, and the Son of man is betrayed into the hands of sinners." Matthew 26:45.

Even as He spoke, they heard the mob approaching. Judas walked at its head, followed closely by the high priest. Jesus turned to His disciples and said, "Rise, let us be going: behold, he is at hand that doth betray me." Verse 46.

From the time of His baptism, Christ had lived under the burden of the world's sins, but on three occasions He literally suffered the paroxysms of death—in the wilderness, in the Garden, and on the cross.

In the wilderness He overcame where Adam failed, but in Gethsemane He tasted death for all humanity. Because of what Christ did there, all mankind was lifted in moral value with God, for His victory in the Garden was for every descendant of Adam.

The question often arises as to how the Saviour could possibly have suffered enough on Passover day to taste death for every man. Obviously an ordinary person could not have done this. No fallen being can ever atone for his own sins, much less for the sins of another. But Christ's purity of character and His sinless life made the difference. Such attributes increased His tolerance for suffering. Man's transgression demanded the suffering of a man, but Christ gave the suffering of a God.

The disciples stood mortified and embarrassed at their Master's conduct in allowing the unruly mob to bind and insult Him. Knowing that He could easily free Himself from the hands of the murderers, they could not understand His actions. Terror-stricken, they fled the scene, leaving the Saviour of the world in the hands of evil men.

First the mob took Him to the house of Annas, the father-in-law of the currently officiating high priest. Formerly the high priest himself, Annas was still an active figure in the Sanhedrin. People believed him to be the voice of God on earth. Annas was overjoyed to see Jesus in custody. He rushed Christ to the palace of the officiating high priest, Caiaphas, where the two priests interrogated and abused Him.

Although it was unlawful to conduct a trial during the night, the hastily assembled Sanhedrin did so because of the need for expediency. They wanted to condemn, try, and execute Jesus before the seven-day Feast of Unleavened Bread began.

Blinded by prejudice and cruelty, they did not recognize that their Passover festival no longer had any purpose since they had rejected Jesus, the antitype of all the types and services of their Jewish ritual. They did not discern that they were about to crucify the One whose blood the Passover lamb prefigured. Little did they realize that the merits of the One they were condemning in such an unjust manner could alone avert God's judgment against all humanity.

The Jewish leaders involved in the conspiracy placed two main charges against Him. The first stated that He had disturbed the peace—an attempt to find favor with the Romans who were having much trouble with insurrection and acts of disobedience among the Jews. The second was that of blasphemy, since Christ had declared Himself to be the Son of God. The latter offense was a Jewish crime punishable by death. The priests used false witnesses and lies to create an appearance of legality to the proceedings, but the trial degenerated into such a disgusting display of vile injustice that even the Romans were ashamed to witness the scene.

It is not difficult to follow the timing of the various events. Chronological evidence in the Gospel accounts indicates that Judas betrayed the Saviour in the Garden around midnight. Trials before the two priests and the process of arraignment before the Sanhedrin took up the next three hours.

After this they treated Christ as a condemned criminal, despite the illegality of the night trial. While He waited for the legal trial at break of day, the priests kept Him in the guardroom just off the courtyard of the palace of the high priest. During the same period Peter denied his Master three times. It was the darkest and the coldest part of the night.

In the guardroom Christ faced the most cruel and inhuman mockery. The roar of voices sounded like that of wild beasts as they persecuted Him. Through it all the Saviour directed no word or even a look of retaliation against His tormentors.

Suddenly, the figure of Judas pressed toward the front of the hall. To the high priest, Caiaphas, he shouted, "He is innocent. Spare Him, O Caiaphas! He has done nothing worthy of death." Judas rushed to the throne of judgment and threw down the thirty pieces of silver Zechariah had seen in vision. (Zechariah 11:12, 13.) Desperately he grasped the robes of the high priest, imploring him to release Jesus. Haughtily the high priest shoved the betrayer from him, and Judas rushed from the hall in despair and hanged himself.

The Gospel writers agree that when morning dawned, the chief priest and elders of the people had Jesus bound and delivered Him to Pontius Pilate, the Roman governor. After another interrogation, the magistrate referred Him to Herod, tetrarch of Galilee.

Neither official had any desire to become involved in condemning this innocent man. Herod, hardened though he was, dared not ratify the charges made against Jesus. Instead, he sent Jesus back to Pilate. Pilate, in turn, sought to have the people choose between Christ and Barabbas, a notorious murderer and criminal, for it was the custom to release a prisoner at that time of year.

But the leaders of the opposition against Christ had made their decision. They could no longer tolerate Jesus the Healer, the Teacher. They determined to silence the Speaker of the Beatitudes. "Away with Him," the people shouted. "Crucify Him! We will not have this Man reign over us!" "Give us Barabbas!" the frenzied mob demanded—Barabbas, the revolutionist, the would-be Messiah who had stopped short of nothing to further his ambitious dreams. The mob considered Barabbas far easier to cope with than Jesus of Nazareth.

Beside him in the judgment hall stood the Man from Nazareth. He watched the mob with a bearing strangely like that of a king, His noble dignity quite unlike that of any human monarch. He was stripped to the waist, the old purple robe the mocking soldiers had placed around Him now removed. A tangled crown of thorns for a diadem encircled His bleeding head.

Bruised, bleeding, faint from the terrible night through which He had passed, He could still look out over the crowd with great compassion. They were His people, His chosen ones. How could He give them up?

But His chosen nation could endure only three and a half years of the Messiah's presence. Purity and holiness could no longer dwell side by side with immorality and selfishness. The incompatibility of it was far too painful.

To Pilate's astonishment the people had chosen to free Barabbas and crucify Jesus. Again and again Pilate tried to save Him, because he recognized a superior Being, an innocent Person. But the magistrate's wavering indecision proved to be his eternal ruin. Pontius Pilate turned the Son of God over to the murderous mob, who cried, "We have no king but Caesar." "His blood be on us, and on our children."

With those prophetic words, the theocracy formed at Sinai ended. God had been their Leader for fifteen centuries, and they had been His people. But now they had made their choice. They had no king but Caesar.

The cowardly judge turned apologetically to Jesus, saying that he was sorry but he could not save Him.

Scourged, insulted, mocked, spat upon, the Son of God remained calm and unmoved. Hatred beat upon Him like waves against a mighty rock. His stately bearing indicated His spiritual relationship with His Father, amazing the rude soldiers and the conniving priests. They saw only pity for themselves in His eyes.

The three trials before Pilate, Herod, and back to Pilate consumed about three hours. Jesus was crucified about nine o'clock in the morning—the hour of the morning sacrifice.

"And it was the third hour, and they crucified him." Mark 15:25. The Jewish and Roman authorities had subjected Him to seven trials in the nine-hour period—twice before priests, twice before the Sanhedrin, twice before Pilate, and once before Herod.

From the third hour in the morning (about nine o'clock) to the sixth hour (noon), Christ endured the most vile abuse and torture to be imagined. (Mark 15:25-34.) He who in modesty shunned all public exposure was completely disrobed and crucified. The psalmist had foretold, "For dogs have compassed me: the assembly of the wicked have inclosed me: they pierced my hands and my feet. . . . They part my garments among them, and cast lots upon my vesture." Psalm 22:16-18.

"And when the sixth hour [midday] was come, there was darkness over the whole land until the ninth hour [about three o'clock]." Mark 15:33. Complete darkness enveloped the cross and the vicinity about it like a funeral pall.

The darkness lasted three hours. A nameless terror took possession of everybody around the cross, and the cursing and reviling came to an abrupt stop. The silence of the grave seemed to have taken over. Priests, rulers, scribes, executioners, the mob—all thought their time of retribution had come.

At the ninth hour (about midafternoon) the darkness lifted, but it still enveloped the Saviour. As He felt the deepest despair of the sinner in being separated from His Father, He lamented, "My God, my God, why hast thou forsaken me?"

There was to be no release from the third paroxysm of death.

# PASSOVER DAY

| Supper | Garden | Trials | Sanhedrin | Mocking | Pilate | Cross | Darkness | Grave |
|--------|--------|--------|-----------|---------|--------|-------|----------|-------|
| | Priests | | | | | | | |
| 6 P.M. 9 P.M. | Midnight | 3 A.M. Trials | | 3 A.M. Trials | 6 A.M. 9 A.M. | | Noon | 3 P.M. 6 P.M. |

Midnight betrayal

Judas

Peter

Thief

Earthquake

Rested from work of redemption

Seven times arraigned—twice before priests, twice before Sanhedrin, twice before Pilate, once before Herod.

| | | | |
|-------------|----------------|-----------|----------------------------------|
| Sunset | Matthew 26:20 | 6-9 P.M. | Supper |
| Garden | Matthew 26:40 | 9-12 P.M. | Garden—tasted death for every man |
| | Mark 14:37, 39, 41 | | |
| Betrayal | Matthew 26:47, 48 | 12-3 A.M. | Trial |
| Morning | Matthew 27:1 | 3-6 A.M. | Mocking—Peter denies |
| | Luke 22:66 | | |
| | Mark 15:1 | 6-9 A.M. | Sanhedrin, Pilate, Herod, Pilate |
| Crucifixion | Mark 15:25 | 9-12 A.M. | Mocking |
| | Luke 23:40-43 | | Thief saved |
| Death | Mark 15:33, 34 | 12-3 P.M. | Darkness—death |
| | Matthew 27:46 | | |
| | Luke 23:44, 46 | | |
| Earthquake | Matthew 27:51 | | |
| Evening | Matthew 27:59, 60 | 3-6 P.M. | In the grave |
| Sunset | Mark 15:42 | | |

These times are approximate, but in general they give an accurate description of the last twenty-four hours Jesus spent upon earth before His death.

# 16

## The Altar of Calvary

THE RELIGION of Christ is the essence of love, kindness, and compassion. Anything else, Satan inspires and fans into action. Imbued with the characteristics of Satan, proud and bigoted zealots will stop at nothing in order to defend their man-made rules and regulations for worship. Hardened as the Roman soldiers were, the morning of Christ's crucifixion they stood amazed at the torture which the Jewish priests and leaders inflicted on Him. The Prisoner would not have lived to reach the cross had they not intervened.

The fact that God sent His Son to the world at a time when the Roman power held sway shows God's wisdom. Had the Jewish leadership possessed full authority, we would not have a history of Christ's life and ministry among men. The priests and rulers, jealous of Him, would have quickly destroyed so formidable a rival. They would have stoned Christ to death on the false accusation of breaking the law of God. The Jews put no one to death by crucifixion. It was a Roman method. The Jews apparently considered anybody executed in such a manner to be especially cursed. (See Deuteronomy 21:23; Galatians 3:13.) Christ died by crucifixion only because the Romans controlled Palestine. If the Jews had stoned Christ, the symbolism of Christ being publicly lifted up before the people—as Moses lifted up the bronze serpent in the Sinai desert—would have failed.

God used the Roman Empire as His instrument to prevent

the record and influence of Christ's life from vanishing or being obscured. The presence of the Roman occupation forces meant that Christ's death would be brought to the attention of thousands from all over the then-known world.

Christ hanging on the cross was the gospel in essence. Groaning under the weight of every man's guilt, feeling to the fullest the wrath of the Father against the sins He assumed responsibility for, Christ was scarcely aware of the added agony that wracked His physical frame. Twice before, in the wilderness and in Gethsemane, Christ had tasted the pangs of death for every man. But Calvary was the ultimate of anguish and suffering, the epitome of woe. Human nature alone would have been inadequate to bear it. Humanity and divinity combined, however, had an infinite capacity for suffering, enough capacity to pay the debt of every sinner in the world.

At Calvary Christ did more than bear man's sins. *He became sin itself.* The vilest and lowest of crimes accumulated in the person of the divine High Priest. The craft of the deceitful and wily Caiaphas, the cruelty of Herod, the treachery of Judas, combined for punishment in Christ.

But the more men hated Him, the more He loved them. When He cried out for His Father to forgive them, that prayer embraced every man who ever lived or would live.

During the fearful ordeal, only the thief acknowledged the crucified Saviour as God, accepting the atonement He was making. Christ's crucifixion crushed and humiliated the disciples and the mother of Jesus. Their fondest dreams had come to what they believed was a most ignominious end.

"We thought He was the Messiah," they wailed.

"We thought it was He who should deliver Israel."

Surely, they reasoned, He would save Himself and come down from the cross—He who had raised the dead before their very eyes, He who had walked on the waters of Galilee. But no, He was dying, and this truth rapidly became a reality to them.

Jesus, weighed down with the sins of the world, felt to the fullest the separation that sin makes between God and man. As He struggled with Satan's temptations, He received no encouragement from Heaven. God did nothing to reassure Christ or to give Him confidence. Three times during His ministry, the voice of God the Father had been heard on earth, testifying that Christ was His beloved Son, but now there was only silence. No comforting angel, no divine presence, sustained Him. The hosts of evil pressed around Him as Heaven stood back and left Him in the hands of the enemy.

Satan had faithfully and consistently followed Christ from the manger to Calvary. Again and again he had met defeat, and now only moments remained in his desperate struggle. If he did not win at once here and now, his loss would be irrevocable.

Demons in the form of men joined the jeering mob to hurl insult after insult against the suffering Saviour. He was supposed to have saved others. Why then, some argued, could He not save Himself? If He was the Messiah, they would believe it only if He came down from the cross. On and on they taunted, but Christ did not yield to the temptations to prove to them that He was truly the Son of God.

The enormous mass of the world's sin had come between the Father and the Son like a great dark cloud. All communion between them had ceased. But Heaven was present. The Father and the holy angels, clothed in the thick darkness that had covered the land, came to the cross to watch the Saviour die. Hidden from the gaze of the curious multitude, Jesus drank the last dregs of the bitter cup.

As *Victim* Jesus suffered great physical torture. The wounds made by the nails in the palms of His hands gaped with the weight of His body, and from His hands and feet blood fell drop by drop to the rock which had been drilled for the base of the cross. Blood flowed from His wounded temples; and as fever mounted in His body, He cried, "I thirst."

As *Victim,* the Son of God died by the hands of those He had come to save. Being made sin for them, He bore their shame and guilt. He paid their penalty at Calvary and then, through His blood, bore all the confessed sins of His people to the sanctuary in heaven. Through the virtue of His shed blood pardon would be registered against the names of penitent believers. But though He was man's Sin Bearer, He was also the sinless Son of God. Though He became sin itself for man in the eyes of God, He was not touched personally with the least taint of corruption.

As *Priest,* Jesus laid down His life voluntarily. He had told His disciples that no man could take it from Him. "I lay it down of myself." (John 10:18.) Although He died to pay a death penalty, He had committed no crime. By virtue of His sin-free blood Heaven would blot out all confessed sins from the record books "when the times of refreshing . . . [should] come." (Acts 3:19.)

As *Priest,* Jesus groaned under the burden of the sins of the world. As the Father hid His face, Jesus felt the anguish and terror that the sinner will feel in the day when all stand before the throne of God. Though His suffering as Victim was terrible, His anguish as Priest was beyond description. It was the sense of His Father's displeasure against sin which crushed from Him the last spark of life. In His bitter despair, He could not see beyond the darkness of death. Bright hope did not

127

display to Him His coming forth a conqueror over death or His Father's acceptance of His great sacrifice. Jesus feared that sin was so offensive in the sight of His Father that He could not be reconciled to His Son. The terrible temptation that His own Father had forever left Him caused Him to cry out on the cross, "My God, my God, why hast thou forsaken me?"

By faith alone Jesus trusted in His Father. In the strange daytime darkness He drained the mysterious cup. "Father, into thy hands I commend my spirit." In submission He said, "It is finished." Faithful to the will of His Father to the end, He had completed His mission on earth. At the same moment the mysterious tearing of the inner veil opened the most holy place of the Temple to public view. The knife slipped from the priest's hand. The sacrificial lamb escaped.

Crucifixion was a slow death, and painful, usually taking two or three days. Yet Christ died in six hours. Then with His last words the darkness which had engulfed the countryside lifted. The Roman soldier who stood at the foot of the cross raised his spear and thrust it into Christ's side. But the Saviour did not feel the stroke of death.

The Bible records that two distinct streams, one of blood, the other of water, poured out of the pierced side. The blood was to wash away the sins of His followers. The water portrays the living water Christ offers, a water signifying Christ's gift of eternal life to man.

The disciples of Jesus mourned, but the angels of God broke into rapturous songs of praise. Heaven sang for joy. The sinner could now be lifted from degradation and ruin, made fit for the kingdom of heaven.

To the surprise of everyone, two important men came to help the frightened disciples in their time of need—Joseph of Arimathaea and Nicodemus, members of the Sanhedrin and prominent men in Israel. Both believed in Jesus' Messiahship, and now they boldly claimed the body of the Saviour. Joseph offered his tomb for Christ's body, and before the end of that eventful day, Jesus rested in the grave.

Christ had yielded up His life beyond the walls of Jerusalem, "outside the camp," where murderers and thieves were executed, thus showing that He died not only for the Jewish people but for the entire world.

Hebrews 13:10-15 declares, "We have an altar [Calvary], whereof they have no right to eat which serve the tabernacle. For the bodies of those beasts, whose blood is brought into the sanctuary by the high priest for sin, are burned without the camp. Wherefore Jesus also, that he might sanctify the people with his own blood, suffered without the gate. Let us go forth therefore unto him without the camp, bearing his reproach. For here have we no continuing city, but we seek one to come. By him therefore let us offer the sacrifice of praise to God continually, that is, the fruit of our lips giving thanks to his name."

Through His death, Jesus destroyed the power of Satan, the power of death. In death, Christ gained the victory. His rising again from the dead made possible the opening of the gates of the grave to all His followers.

He buried the sins of all who will accept Him as a personal Saviour. The Father has laid man's transgressions where none but His own eye can discern them. Just as He hid His face from the innocence of Jesus, so He will hide His eyes from the guilt of the believing sinner because of the righteousness imputed to him.

Man's fate hangs on the events of the cross. Christ's crucifixion will occupy the minds of the redeemed through all eternity. Mankind will never fully comprehend the amazing love of God revealed in His atonement at the altar of Calvary, but each fresh search will bring new revelations of Christ's character.

The emancipation papers of the race have been signed with the blood of Jesus, and now we are prisoners of hope. Heaven is accessible to every man who will accept the freely offered gift. It is our privilege to plead Christ's atoning sacrifice for our pardon, our justification, and our sanctification.

"And every creature which is in heaven, and on the earth, and under the earth, and such as are in the sea, and all that are in them, heard I saying, Blessing, and honour, and glory, and power, be unto him that sitteth upon the throne, and unto the Lamb for ever and ever." Revelation 5:13.

It will be recalled that in the sanctuary on earth, the priest completed atonement in three phases, each dependent on the other. The first one took place in the court, the second in the holy place, the third in the most holy place. The complete disposition of sin could not be accomplished until the Day of Atonement.

The antitypical atonement is also completed in three steps. First, Jesus, the divine High Priest, made a sacrificial atonement for man's sins in the court (the earth). He completed one phase of His priesthood when He died on the cross for the fallen human race.

The second step He accomplished in the first apartment of the heavenly sanctuary, where for 1,800 years He ministered for His people by shedding the benefits of His sacrifice on all true believers. There He consummated another phase of His atoning work by ministering the benefits of His sacrificial death before the Father. This work is as essential as His death on the cross, for only as Christ's sacrifice is put to man's credit and account can man benefit from it.

In the second apartment, Christ began the third part of the atonement, a phase of His priesthood still in progress. Even today Heaven is determining who has benefited from the great offering. Jesus in His work as Priest and Judge is making a perfect expiatory atonement. Sins are being blotted from the record books of heaven. Names are being accepted. Other names are being rejected. Without the final phase of the atonement, the first two would be valueless, for the record of sin would still stand between man and God.

On the altar of Calvary, Jesus made the only offering that is of value with Deity. There Jesus fulfilled the conditions of the atonement. With the incense of His perfect life and the blood of His perfect offering, He ascended victoriously as our Substitute and Surety to the throne of God to continue His work of reconciliation.

# 17

## Christ, the Sinless Sin Bearer

THE INCARNATION of Christ is a mystery which man with his limited mind and experience can never fully understand. Heaven termed the humanity of Christ "that holy thing" because no other has ever come into the world under similar circumstances. The Record states precisely the manner of Mary's conception, and her willing acceptance of it. "And the angel answered and said unto her, The Holy Ghost shall come upon thee, and the power of the Highest shall overshadow thee: therefore also that holy thing which shall be born of thee shall be called the Son of God." Luke 1:35.

When the Prince of peace left heaven, He declared, "Sacrifice and offering thou wouldest not, but a body hast thou prepared me, . . . to do thy will, O God." Hebrews 10:5-7.

Christ, as He lived on earth, was a singular combination of man and God. To become human, He clothed His divinity with humanity, yet He never ceased to also be God. It is, of course, unthinkable that Deity could dwell in a body combined with sinful human nature. Sin cannot exist in the presence of God, and although He shared man's physical degeneration, He did not possess man's spiritual alienation from and rebellion against God. Neither did He sin by thought, deed, or action. He accepted only the human physical condition as it existed after four thousand years, becoming tired, hungry, and weak like any other human being.

It has been pointed out that Christ possessed two natures,

that of a man and that of God. He exhibited a perfect humanity, combined with Deity. By preserving each of the two natures distinct, He has given the world a representation of the
character of God and the character of a perfect man. He
showed man what God is, and what man may become—Godlike in character.

Another situation difficult to understand is why Christ did
not partake of the sinful tendencies inherited by all the other
descendants of Adam. To comprehend this fundamental fact,
one must consider the nature of sin and the contrast of man in
his fallen condition with man before he sinned.

Primal man came from the hand of God perfect in every
sense of the word. He had no sin, no evil tendency. But when
Adam accepted Satan's leadership and did the exact thing God
told him not to do, he immediately fell in league with the
tempter. Now he had a fallen, sinful nature.

Having tempted man to sin, Satan declared that he controlled the earth. He referred to himself as the prince of the
world. Having shaped to his own nature the father and mother
of the human race, Satan planned to establish his empire here.
He claimed that they had chosen him as their sovereign.
Through his control of men, he held dominion over the world.
Man thus became separated from God.

Adam's posterity shared in his sin as they were born into
his exile from God. As a result, all have become passive sinners—*passive* because it was Adam's sin which brought about
the alienation of all men. At birth Adam's posterity are all
sinners in need of a Saviour.

Passive sin gives rise to active sin, or that which a person
actively commits. Men sin because they have sinful natures. All
men are born into a state which automatically classifies them
as sinners. Adam's fall resulted in total depravity. His total

nature was at enmity with God. This was graphically illustrated when Adam's first male child became the first murderer.

When Adam sinned, he at once came under the influence of Satan. He was no longer a free moral agent able to choose right or wrong. Under Satan's power he was an abject slave, incapable of sensing sin or righteousness. He had no desire for holiness. Defiantly accusing God of causing his fall, he joined Satan in rebellion against God. His nature conformed to that of the powerful mind which held him captive.

As a result of his transgression, he and his posterity have become Satan's captives. Were it not for Someone stronger than the devil, man would be doomed to hopeless servitude. Man's nature in sin is preternatural—nonnatural, abnormal. The power that will restore him must be supernatural.

The mystery of sin and the mystery of the atonement are indeed challenging subjects, which the human mind has difficulty fathoming. The sinful nature with which all men except Christ were born is something more dangerous and evil than humanity can comprehend or accept. Man—even the non-Christian—can overcome his developed bad habits, but he cannot escape from the sinful nature which he has received from Adam. The Apostle Paul summarized the problem when he said, "Wretched man that I am—who shall deliver me from the body of this death?" Romans 7:24.

Because of the nature man inherits at birth, no amount of obedience to the law will entitle him to enter the kingdom of heaven. *It is not so much what he does, but what he is, that is important.* Nothing that man can do apart from accepting Christ's atonement has any value in making peace with God.

No matter how good a person's deeds are, the sinful nature is always there, and it cannot dwell in the presence of God. Until Christ binds the source of evil and puts him in chains, mortal man will always have Satan's hellish shadow cast over him. It is only by faith that man can be free—faith in Him who has promised to make you perfect "through the blood of the everlasting covenant."

Because the potential human race existed in Adam, his transgression caused all humanity to share in his guilt. Adam could not pass to his offspring something he did not have— righteousness. As for Christ, God was His Father, so He did not share in the passive sin which the first man passed to his posterity.

Sin is not transferred as a genetic factor. The genes or chromosomes do not carry it, yet it is in sense an inherited trait. Sin is passed on like an inheritance of royalty or slavery. The children of slaves become slaves because their parents are slaves. In some societies if a freeman legally marries a slave, the children are free thereafter, but if there is no legal pronouncement of marriage, the children are still slaves. Morphologically, such offspring would be the same, but legally different.

Christ was the Son of God, and God publicly proclaimed Him as such. "This is my beloved Son, in whom I am well pleased." Thus, although born of a mother with a sinful nature, He was freeborn and sinless.

Sin may be considered a divine pronouncement. It is a separation from God, passed down upon the race from Adam. It is like a birthright handed down from the father, but not biologically.

Since the entire race was in Adam at his creation, we all come under condemnation because of his sin in the light of the holy law.

As with slavery, royalty is conveyed usually in a similar manner. When Edward VIII of Great Britain abdicated his throne in 1936, he publicly declared his "irrevocable determination to renounce the throne," for himself and for his descendants forever. His descendants, if any, could never inherit what he had given away. A new king was crowned, and his children became the lawful heirs to the throne.

Adam, king of Eden, abdicated his throne forever when he violated willingly the legal conditions by which he might retain his right to the kingdom of this world. Satan gained the throne by trickery. Adam yielded him his mind and body in abject servitude. Under this hypnotic power Adam's mind became conformed to that of the devil. He fell just as surely as Satan had fallen. His posterity could not inherit what he had forfeited. They had been sold into slavery forever, and their natural inheritance was a mind attuned to that of the slave master.

On the other hand, Christ's inheritance was not that of a mind attuned to Satan. His mind was pure and holy, for at His incarnation, the Holy Spirit was His Father—"Thou art my Son; this day have I begotten thee."

Christ was the second Adam; He began His work where the first Adam began. The first Adam did not begin his life under the dominion of Satan, nor did the second Adam. He came to earth as a human being and as a representative of man, to show in the controversy with Satan that man as he came from the hand of the Creator, in union with the Father and Son, could obey every divine requirement.

What did Christ receive from Mary?

He entered humanity through her. She was the cradle, the vehicle for Him to become human. From her He became genetically of the line of Abraham.

After Christ assumed human nature, He faced temptation like any other human being. Christ could have sinned. He could have fallen. But He had no evil inclination. He accepted human heredity in that He was smaller and weaker physically than the first Adam, but such a condition is not sin. He was a perfect man in which the union of God and man fused into one holy Being. In every respect He was perfect, just as the first Adam was in the beginning.

As one considers the nature of Christ during His incarnation, he will encounter some Bible texts seemingly at variance with the Bible's general theme that Christ was without sin at His birth. First Corinthians 5:21 offers one example: "For he hath made him to be sin for us, who knew no sin; that we might be made the righteousness of God in him."

The Scriptural evidence to the contrary is too overwhelming for the careful Bible student to believe that Christ was born with a sinful nature, with tendencies toward evil. If such were the case, one sinful being could atone for another.

When, then, did Christ become "sin for us"?

The Scriptures give just one instance of a direct transfer of sin to the Saviour, an event which occurred at His baptism, for at that time John declared, "Behold the Lamb of God, which taketh away the sin of the world." John 1:29.

Notice that the statement includes all sin: Adam's sin, with its implied universal guilt to all mankind, as well as the entirety of personal sins of the past, present, and future. Christ accepted all of it when John baptized Him at the Jordan. His former life of peacefulness in the carpenter shop came to an end. As His public ministry began, He entered into a more active warfare with Satan.

Of the vast throng present at the Jordan, few besides John discerned the heavenly vision. Yet the solemnity of the divine Presence rested upon the assembly. People stood, gazing at Christ, noting the light that bathed His form. It was then

137

that the voice of God first proclaimed Him to be the Son of God.

It is not easy to comprehend that a sinless Being could and would become sin for man. The import of it is overwhelming, for, by assuming responsibility for humanity's sins, He at once became guilty of every sin in the world that had ever been committed, or would ever be committed. Every terrible deed from the time of Adam's transgression on down to today with its Auschwitz and its immorality of every kind rested upon "him . . . who knew no sin." He stood guilty before His own holy law. Condemned as a criminal, He must die for the sins of the world.

The Bible record further states that Jesus, after His baptism, went immediately into the Palestinian wilderness to face the devil's temptations. The terrible guilt of the world weighed Him down. Previous to the baptism, there appears no record of His being sin laden in any way during His life in Galilee.

In the wilderness, Christ won a victory which every believer can claim as his own. Although He endured an agonizing fast of nearly six weeks, it was not alone the gnawing pangs of intense hunger which made His sufferings so severe. In addition, the guilt resulting from the sins of the world pressed heavily upon Him. (See chapters 19 and 20.)

# 18

# "Thou Art My Priest"

MANY SIMILARITIES exist between the life of Christ and the human priest who served in the early history of the world. As pointed out earlier, the priest inherited his office, was born to his position. The patriarchal priest—the father—was the head of the family, and upon his death the eldest son replaced him. The Levitical priesthood was more restrictive in who would serve as priest. Only the tribe of Levi ascended to the priesthood.

"But thou shalt appoint the Levites over the tabernacle of testimony, and over all the vessels thereof, and over all things that belong to it: they shall bear the tabernacle, and all the vessels thereof; and they shall minister unto it, and shall encamp round about the tabernacle." Numbers 1:50. Aaron's sons and descendants, however, were the only ones ordained to participate as priests in the sacrificial service of the Tabernacle. (See Exodus 28.)

No one else, no matter how much he aspired to the position, could possibly attain to the office. He had to be born to the priesthood. The term of service for all priests except the high priest extended from the age of thirty until he became fifty years old. Anointed at thirty, the priest retired at fifty. "From thirty years old and upward until fifty years old shalt thou number them; all that enter in to perform the service, to do the work in the tabernacle of the congregation." Numbers 4:23.

Christ was appointed to His office as High Priest by God. (Hebrews 5:4-6, 10.) He was born to be Priest of the Most High, the High Priest over the house of God, the head of "an unchangeable priesthood," the intercessor at the right hand of God the Father.

Like the Levitical priest, Christ began His public ministry at the age of thirty, when the Holy Ghost anointed Him at the Jordan. "And Jesus himself began to be about thirty years of age, being (as was supposed) the son of Joseph." Luke 3:23.

But Christ, of course, did not belong to the Levitical priesthood. He had descended neither from Aaron nor from the tribe of Levi. Being of the tribe of Judah, He had no right to be a priest of the earthly Tabernacle. Rather, God called Him to serve in the pattern of the patriarchal priest, Melchizedek.

Despite the many similarities, there were differences between Christ's Priesthood and that of the patriarchal and Levitical priesthoods. The human priest had limits of age and succession. When he retired or died, another priest took his place. But the priesthood of Melchizedek lasted forever, without succession.

Hebrews 7:3 states that Melchizedek was "without father, without mother, without descent, having neither beginning of days, nor end of life; but made like unto the Son of God; abideth a priest continually." Apparently the passage means that no record exists of the lineage of Melchizedek. But the statement has an additional and more important significance. The human priest had to be born into a genealogical line possessing the right to serve in the priesthood. Christ, however, became man's Priest outside of any lineage. He had promised and waited to be Priest since before the earth's creation. In Hebrews 7:7, Paul declared, "And without all contradiction, the less is blessed of the better," showing that Christ's Priesthood

140

has the greatest importance to man.

Paul spoke of a change in the priesthood, a change in the law regarding the choosing of the priest. The Hebrew priest came from the tribe of Levi, but Christ was called of God. The patriarchal and Levitical law appointed limited, imperfect men priests, but Christ's Priesthood has "the power of an endless life." (Hebrews 7:16.)

Unlike the other forms of priesthood which changed as occasion brought about a need, Christ's office of priesthood never alters. "But this man, because he continueth ever, hath an unchangeable priesthood." Hebrews 7:24.

The Levitical priest served in the earthly sanctuary, but Christ's sanctuary is in heaven.

God's declaration to Christ, "Thou art my Son," appears several times in the New Testament. Its proclamation at His baptism (Luke 3:22) and His resurrection (Acts 13:33) gives the statement great significance. Several times Paul used the phrase in the Book of Hebrews to present the Priesthood of Christ. The atonement required a priest, a mediator, who was both God and man. Only such a being could serve as a bridge between mankind in his fallen condition and God.

Paul meticulously discussed Christ's Priesthood with special emphasis on its basis. After discussing the foundation of this office, he concluded his arguments in Hebrews 8:1, 2: "Now of the things we have spoken this is the sum: We have such an high priest, who is set on the right hand of the throne of the Majesty in the heavens; a minister of the sanctuary, and of the true tabernacle, which the Lord pitched, and not man."

The apostle recognized the fundamental fact that Christ as Priest of the Most High must necessarily have both human and divine attributes. First he established the Deity of Christ in the first chapter of Hebrews. He presented the evidence that

He is the Son of God. In the eighth verse he quoted from the Psalms, "Thy throne, O God, is for ever and ever: a sceptre of righteousness is the sceptre of thy kingdom." Then in the tenth verse he emphasized Christ's role as Creator: "And, Thou, Lord, in the beginning hast laid the foundation of the earth; and the heavens are the works of thine hands."

The second chapter of Hebrews deals with Christ's humanity. That Christ was actually a real man in every sense of the word cannot be denied. "For verily he took not on him the nature of angels; but he took on him the seed of Abraham." Hebrews 2:16. An earlier verse mentions man's original state: "Thou madest him a little lower than the angels; thou crownedst him with glory and honour, and didst set him over the works of thy hands." Hebrews 2:7.

The next verses, commenting on man's fall, contain an element of sadness: "Thou hast put all things in subjection under his feet. For in that he put all in subjection under him, he left nothing that is not put under him. *But now we see not yet all things put under him.* But we see Jesus, *who was made a little lower than the angels* for the suffering of death, *crowned with glory and honour;* that he by the grace of God should taste death for every man." Verses 8, 9.

The passage presents a description of the first and the second Adam. Both had bodies prepared for them by God. "A body hast thou prepared me," Christ said. (Hebrews 10:5.) God made both a little lower than the angels—Christ at His incarnation, Adam at his creation—and both received glory and honor. The first man fell from his lofty position—"but now we see not yet all things put under him." The description of Jesus, however, presents the wonders of the atonement: "That he by the grace of God should taste death for every man."

No angel could possibly have taken Christ's place in the redemption plan, for they are created beings and are unequal with God. Man had broken God's law, the transcript of His character. It required the sacrifice of one equal with the law. Only a perfect character could atone for man's transgression. God's only Son was equal to the task set before Him.

The atonement, the everlasting covenant, required the service of a priest. God promised to accept the service of a divine-human priest. The conditions necessary for atonement must be met in order for the prerogatives of justice and mercy to stand. The justice of the immutability of the law must be revealed; the Priest, Sin Bearer, must die to demonstrate mercy to the fallen race.

When God declared, "Thou art my Son, this day have I begotten thee," He was also saying, Thou art My Priest, "thou art a priest for ever after the order of Melchisedec." Hebrews 5:6.

# 19

# Christ's Baptism and the Atonement

"JOHN DID baptize in the wilderness, and preach the baptism of repentance for the remission of sins. And there went out unto him all the land of Judaea, and they of Jerusalem, and were all baptized of him in the river of Jordan, confessing their sins." Mark 1:4, 5.

"Then cometh Jesus from Galilee to Jordan unto John, to be baptized of him. But John forbad him, saying, I have need to be baptized of thee, and comest thou to me? And Jesus answering said unto him, Suffer it to be so now: for thus it becometh us to fulfil all righteousness. Then he suffered him. And Jesus, when he was baptized, went up straightway out of the water: and, lo, the heavens were opened unto him, and he saw the Spirit of God descending like a dove, and lighting upon him: and lo a voice from heaven, saying, This is my beloved Son, in whom I am well pleased." Matthew 3:13-17.

Multitudes had flocked to the banks of the river that day, waiting in turn as publicans, soldiers, criminals, and others stepped into the water one by one, confessing dark tales of crime and sins of every hue. But why should the Son of God, who needed no repentance, submit to the humiliating rite, especially since the ceremony was a confession of guilt?

Christ's act amazed none as much as John. Filled with awe, he watched Christ approach, feeling himself in the presence of Divinity. He knew Jesus was the one about whom he had prophesied, "There cometh one mightier than I after me, the latchet of whose shoes I am not worthy to stoop down and unloose." Mark 1:7.

As Jesus made His strange request, John shrank back, exclaiming, "I have need to be baptized of thee, and comest thou to me?" Matthew 3:14.

No confession escaped the lips of the Nazarene, for no act of disobedience, no thought of impurity, no deed of selfishness had marred the record of His life. His character was a living demonstration of perfection from the day of His birth. Yet Jesus identified Himself with the sinners standing on the banks of the river, and asked to be baptized. He silenced John's protests, saying, "Thus it becometh us to fulfil all righteousness." Verse 15.

Was the baptism merely an example for repentant believers to follow, or was it an essential part of the atonement? What was the full significance of the event? How would it "fulfil all righteousness"?

Leviticus 10:17 points out the inseparable relationship between the priest and lamb in the atonement. In Abraham's time, the priest laid the sins of the family on the innocent animal victim. Christ, acting as the world's sacrificial Lamb, assumed humanity's sins. It was the only way that He could provide the captives held in Satan's power with a means of escape. He must meet the enemy as man's representative and conquer him, winning a victory over every temptation. Man could not overcome temptation by himself. Christ would put His triumph to their credit, for in taking their sins upon Himself, He would be their Substitute. But first He must identify Himself with those He had come to save.

As the sinners went down into the water, confessing their evil deeds, Christ knew that their repentance could never be deep enough. Their strongest faith was only feebleness. He must do the work for them, for they could not do it by themselves.

After coming up from the water, Jesus bowed in prayer on the banks of the Jordan. Laden with man's sins, He prayed for each person. He knew how hard it would be for men to accept the gift of salvation, and He pleaded with the Father for power to overcome man's unbelief. He pleaded, too, for a sign that God would accept humanity through Him.

When the heavens opened then and beams of glory descended from the throne of the Father, the Holy Spirit in the form of a dove rested over the head of the Saviour, bathing Him with rays of light.

It was clear that God had recognized Christ as man's representative and that He had anointed Him for the work He must begin to do in freeing men from Satan's power. "That word, I say, ye know, which was published throughout all Judaea, and began from Galilee, after the baptism which John preached; how God anointed Jesus of Nazareth with the Holy Ghost and with power: who went about doing good, and healing all that were oppressed of the devil; for God was with him." Acts 10:37, 38.

From the opened heavens came peals of thunder, and the Father's voice proclaimed Him His Son.

Satan witnessed Christ's baptism. He heard the voice of God echoing through the earth. He knew that man now had a sure access to heaven, and hatred greater than before filled his heart. God's voice sounded a death knell to him, for he knew that God could give men the moral power to overcome temptations. Satan braced himself for the contest with the second Adam. He had his entire kingdom to lose. If he did not overcome man's Representative, he would be destroyed by Him.

As for Jesus, He now stood in a vastly different position than He had previously. The Sinless One must now feel the shame of sin. As a human being, He would bear the burden of man's guilt. A new and important era lay ahead.

Just how He could feel the guilt and shame of sin is beyond human understanding. Jesus had become sin for the race.

God would accept the prayers of mankind made through the name of Jesus. The continued, persistent prayer of faith would bring the knowledge and strength to withstand whatever assaults Satan tried to advance.

John the Baptist represented the Levitical priesthood. His father, Zacharias, was ministering in the holy place of the sanctuary when the angel revealed that the prophet was to be born for a special mission. With its completion, John pointed to the baptized Saviour and proclaimed in a loud voice, "Behold the Lamb of God, which taketh away the sin of the world." As the lamb in the Hebrew sacrificial system had the people's sins placed on it, so did Christ, the antitypical Lamb, assume upon Himself the sins of Adam and Eve and every person born since. He knew the price it would cost to redeem the human family from the hands of Satan. Being the final sacrificial Lamb, He would have to die to make the atonement between God and man. But His repentance, baptism, and death—all made in the name of and for man—would satisfy God's broken law and make man acceptable before God.

# 20

# Atonement in the Wilderness

"AND JESUS being full of the Holy Ghost returned from Jordan, and was led by the Spirit into the wilderness, being forty days tempted of the devil. And in those days he did eat nothing: and when they were ended, he afterward hungered." Luke 4:1, 2.

The Holy Spirit led Him into a dreary and desolate wilderness. Bearing the guilt of the entire world, He must suffer not the mildest test, but the most severe temptations that the devil could conceive. He must settle Adam's debt first, before He could free those Satan held in bondage.

The Redeemer must take the place of Adam, who had fallen. Only thus could redemption succeed. *With the sins of the world upon Him,* Jesus must go over the ground where Adam had stumbled. His test was much greater than Adam's in the Garden of Eden. *Jesus would overcome on man's account,* and conquer the tempter, that, through His obedience, His purity of character and steadfast integrity, His righteousness could be ascribed to man.

It is not possible for man to sense the strength of Satan's temptations to the Son of God. Satan used every temptation man faces, and Christ suffered in as much greater degree as His own character was superior to that of sinful man.

Christ could never accomplish the atonement without *suffering,* for man was a debtor to the law. Christ, by His suffering, would pay the debt. But how much would be needed to pay for the accumulated guilt of the world? It would take the suffering of Deity and humanity combined, for human nature alone was inadequate to bear the inconceivable mountain of sin which would almost crush the Saviour. Humanity and Deity together "suffered being tempted" (Hebrews 2:18).

As soon as the long fast began, Satan appeared with his temptations. Every moment of the forty days he attempted to break down Christ's resistance. He came, enshrouded in light, declaring that he was one of the angels from the throne of God, sent to encourage Him and relieve Him of His suffering.

He attempted to make Christ believe that God did not require Him to actually experience the period of self-denial He knew lay ahead of Him. Satan spoke convincingly that he had come to deliver the message that God wanted only proof of His willingness to go through with it, that, like Abraham, Christ had undergone a test to show His perfect obedience.

The being further professed to be the angel who had seized the hand of Abraham as the patriarch stood ready to sacrifice Isaac. Now he had come to save the life of Jesus. God the Father did not consider it necessary for Him to endure painful hunger and a possible death from starvation. Satan would help Him complete the plan of salvation.

Since Christ knew Satan's history of lying, it required even more self-control to listen to him and not rebuke him at once as the insulting deceiver he was. But Satan felt confident that the Son of God would give him a chance to take advantage of Him, for Christ was in a weakened condition and torn by mental agony. Satan planned to twist Christ's statements and certain promises found in Scripture to trip Him, summoning also the fallen angels to help him.

Since it is through the power of perverted appetite that Satan holds man largely under his control, and since in his own strength man cannot break vicious habits and weaknesses, Jesus came to do it for him.

Adam was not even hungry when Eve tempted him with the forbidden fruit. He stood in the strength of perfect humanity. But Christ's fast of nearly six weeks left Him weak and emaciated when Satan engaged Him in earth's most desperate struggle. Jesus had reached the limit of His human endurance. One more day of fasting might well have found Him dead.

Not only hunger caused His suffering, but a sense of guilt for the world's indulgences pressed upon His divine soul. "For he hath made him to be sin for us, who knew no sin; that we might be made the righteousness of God in him." 2 Corinthians 5:21.

Despite His human limitations and with the terrible weight of humanity's sins crushing Him, He withstood the pressures which Satan put upon Him. He did not succumb to the most dangerous temptation man faces. If only man could overcome the enticement of appetite, he could conquer on every other point.

Many have pointed out that intemperance lies at the foundation of all the moral evils known to man. Christ began His redemptive work just where man's ruin began. The indulgence of appetite caused the fall of humanity's first parents. In redemption Christ had as His first task the denial of appetite.

During the forty-day fast the Father had sustained Jesus. Communion with heavenly agencies had lifted Him above the pangs of His hunger. In vision, He saw what He must do to free men from the tyranny of Satan. Jesus would heal the sick, comfort the discouraged, and offer spiritual liberty to sin's captives. He would show men that He would not set up the great earthly kingdom for which their selfish hearts yearned, but a spiritual kingdom.

## The First Victory

At the end of the forty days the vision faded and Christ's physical strength dropped to its lowest ebb. His whole being yearned for nourishment. It was the moment Satan had waited for.

The first Adam had succumbed easily in Eden. Understandably Satan had confidence that the same power he used then would bring the emaciated second Adam under his control. Satan had harassed Jesus from birth, and it enraged him that as yet he had found no means to bring Him under his control. Not even in thought had Jesus responded to his temptations. But now Satan had hope of victory. In such a weakened physical and mental condition, surely Christ would succumb.

Still in his disguise as an angel from the Father's throne, he attempted to confuse the mind of Christ with his brilliance and beauty. "*If* you are God's Son," he said, "You have the power to turn these stones into bread. Just speak the word!"

Satan spoke a fact. Jesus *could* turn the stones into bread, for He was the Creator of the universe. The temptation was powerful. His human body felt pain and hunger. He longed for food, and it was just a word away. Christ stood at His symbolic tree of knowledge of good and evil. As the second Adam, if He should fail the test, the whole world would be lost.

Satan questioned the deity of Christ, subtly suggesting that the Father surely would not leave His Son in such a deplorable condition. Jesus did not debate the issue with him. To do so would be to place Himself in jeopardy, giving Satan the advantage.

The first Adam in Eden had made the mistake of attempt-

151

ing to reason with the enemy. Satan's ability to reason and debate had a hypnotic influence over man, and the rebellious angel attempted to turn this power on Christ. But after Christ replied only by quoting Scripture, he knew that he had no chance of victory.

Satan has greater intelligence than any human being. No man can hope to win an argument with him. But when a person quotes Scripture, he gains access to the infinite wisdom of God. To every suggestion Jesus replied, "It is written." His human nature alone could never have borne the test, but His humanity and deity combined brought Him off more than victor.

"It is written," Jesus said, "Man shall not live by bread alone." Matthew 4:4.

He did not doubt His Father's love for a moment. When God wished Him to have food, He would send it. Christ had not placed Himself in His present position of His own accord. He had come to the Palestinian wilderness in obedience to the directing of God's Spirit, and He was willing to die of starvation if that was the will of the Father.

Christ's trial relative to appetite became an example for man in self-denial. This long fast revealed the sinfulness of the things in which professed Christians often indulge. More important, the salvation of man hung in the balance, and the trial of Christ in the wilderness would decide man's eternal fate. Christ won out over His appetite, thus pointing to the fact that man had a chance to overcome his sinful nature. Had Christ failed, man would have remained bound by the power of appetite, trapped by indulgences which he lacked the moral power to resist.

Jesus lifted humanity in the scale of moral value with God, a situation impossible for man to understand. Nor can he realize how much he loses in the conflict with Satan by yielding to the power of perverted appetite. The devil knows that any physical indulgence that brings weakness to the body will also bring confusion to the mind.

By His own example, Jesus has taught man that he can indulge appetite and passion only at the peril of his soul. Satan confidently knows that he can hold man securely in his power as long as he dulls reason and conscience by the use of stimulants, narcotics, and drugs. Even the overindulgence of wholesome food can bring disease upon the body and confusion to the mind. But *by faith* in Christ's victory, the Christian can conquer such weaknesses. He must appropriate Christ's victory as his. Through Him man can overcome sin. To try apart from Him will end in failure. The Christian must align his strength with the strength of God.

## The Second Victory

Eager to impress Christ with his superior strength, Satan picked Him up bodily and carried Him to Jerusalem, where he set Him on the height of the Temple. He now had set the stage for his second masterpiece of delusion. Again he began by questioning Christ's deity, urging Him to throw Himself down from the pinnacle in order to demonstrate His confidence in the Father. Appearing as an angel, he glibly quoted the Scriptures, even as Christ had done earlier. But although Satan can tempt, he cannot force man to sin. Unless Jesus complied willingly, the deceiver could not gain victory. Faith must let go before Satan can control the mind.

Jesus replied without hesitation. "It is written, . . . Thou shalt not tempt the Lord thy God," He said. Not for a moment would He place Himself in danger to prove whether or not

His Father loved Him. To do so would have been presumption of the worst sort. A vast and important difference exists between presumption and the confidence resulting from faith.

Satan, of course, intended to confuse the great Mediator into manifesting His divine power. He wanted Jesus to put on a startling display of the ability of His Father to preserve Him from injury. Why not, Satan proposed, have Christ appear in His real character and establish beyond doubt His right to the confidence and faith of the people? Why not boldly declare Himself to be the Saviour of the world?

If Christ had done as Satan suggested and given proof of His power to free Himself from His torment, He would have broken the covenant He had with His Father to be a *probationer* in behalf of the human race.

Adam was not deceived by the serpent, as Eve had been. He had no excuse to transgress God's positive command against eating the forbidden fruit. His wife had sinned, and he did not know what would become of her. Adam was a troubled man, sad and uncertain. Doubts arose in his mind as to whether or not to believe God's warning about eating the fruit. *Now* the second Adam had come to earth to prove that God always means exactly what He says, that man could not deviate in the slightest, and that should he depart at all from the will of Deity, he would destroy himself.

Weak, faint from hunger, and perched at a dizzying height on the Temple, Christ had no way to escape from the pinnacle without help. At a word, angels would have borne Him to safety. But again, had He called for aid not readily available to man, He would not have set a perfect pattern for man to follow. Christ could never have served as the great Mediator.

Presumption is the counterfeit of faith. It claims God's promises of aid or protection and then uses them to excuse transgression. Presumption led Adam and Eve to disobey God, all the time believing that His great love would save them from the consequences of their sin. Genuine faith will comply with the conditions laid down by God.

Balanced on the precarious height of the Temple pinnacle, Jesus, as man's Substitute, demonstrated perfect confidence and trust. Through Him God the Father accounts human faith to be perfect and accepts the Christian as though he had never doubted His word, never deviated from His wishes. Christ suffered as a human being, knowing that it was not God's will that He exercise His divine power in His own behalf. Because of His innocence, He felt Satan's assaults even more keenly.

## The Third Victory

Satan's rage and anger because of his second defeat is understandable. He became so upset that he openly revealed his identity, shedding his role of angel sent to help the suffering Saviour. Announcing himself as the god of the earth, he took Jesus in his arms again and carried him to the top of a high mountain. There he performed a miracle, causing a vision of all the kingdoms of the world to pass before Christ's eyes.

All evidence of sin and disobedience was hidden. The panorama before Him was one of unsurpassed beauty and loveliness. There were the marbled palaces and golden-spired temples of earth's most majestic cities. Gardens and fields intermingled with orchards laden with the bounties of nature. Still weak from hunger, still suffering from His stay in the desolate wilderness, Christ must have found the sight dazzling.

Satan told him smugly, "These are mine, and I will give them all to You, everything which lies before You, in exchange for one small consideration. I ask simply that You acknowledge my supremacy. Then I shall relinquish my throne and kingdom." He spoke eloquently of how Christ had no need to continue in His humiliating manner. If He would only bow down and worship Satan, all would be His.

Jesus turned His eyes wearily from the scene below Him. Satan's boldness called for decided action. The majesty of divinity flashed through the frail mantle of humanity, and Jesus cried, "Get thee behind me, Satan: for it is written, Thou shalt worship the Lord thy God, and him only shalt thou serve." Luke 4:8.

Satan had no choice now but to withdraw. He felt anger, humiliation, and frustration.

Christ's victory was as complete as had been Adam's failure. In the second Adam, all mankind stood triumphant. When man accepts Jesus as his Substitute, God looks upon him as though he himself had successfully resisted the trials in the wilderness.

Having now exhausted the last of His physical strength in the conflict with the enemy, Christ fell dying to the ground. But Jesus had settled Adam's account. He had lifted the mortgage that Satan held on the souls of men. Angels of God came to the dying Saviour, bringing Him nourishment and comfort.

# 21

# The New Birth

WHAT DOES it mean to be born again, and thus be justified by faith? Many professed followers of Christ, fluent on most of the great Bible doctrines, find it difficult to answer the question. Even the great reformer John Wesley was active in Christian service for many years before he understood what it means to be justified by faith.

The story is told that once when he was ill and some thought that he was dying, a friend asked him, "On what do you base your hope of eternal life?"

"I have used my best endeavors to serve God!" the preacher replied promptly.

The friend appeared not satisfied with the response, and Wesley was surprised. He began to ask himself whether or not his activities and endeavors were sufficient grounds for hope. Unfortunately he had nothing else in which to trust.

He thought back over the years. Since his youth he had served God faithfully. He had fasted, prayed, and lived a life of strict self-denial, giving up the comforts and pleasures which other men enjoyed. He had donated all he had to help the poor. Furthermore, he had spent hours at a time on his knees in prayer, making a dedicated effort to subdue the evils of his natural inclinations. Wesley's life had been a noble example for others to follow, and now as he lay dying, he had no regrets for having spent himself for the Lord.

But what did his friend mean by his questions? Wasn't

his record good enough recommendation for heaven? He had done his best. What more could God require? Fortunately, God spared his life until he had an opportunity to learn the meaning of justification by faith.

When Wesley sailed to America sometime later, a violent storm came up. The boat was in grave danger of sinking. Angry waves swept over the decks. The howling wind split the mainsail into pieces. Above the gale one could hear the screaming of the terrified passengers. In all the commotion, Wesley noticed a small group of Moravian believers from Germany sitting calmly, singing a hymn. He watched in amazement. Even the children appeared composed and quiet.

When at last the storm passed, he approached one of the Moravians. "You were not afraid?" he queried.

The man said he was not.

"But were not your women and children afraid?" John Wesley seemed to seek confirmation in words of what his eyes had already witnessed.

"No, our women and children are not afraid to die," came the answer.

Later the humble Moravians instructed the great Wesley, helping him arrive at a clearer understanding of Bible faith. At last he saw the correct foundation on which to base his hope of eternal life.

To understand the doctrine of spiritual rebirth, one must take into consideration the fact that man is Satan's lawful captive, naturally inclined to follow his suggestions. It can readily be understood then that only supernatural power can change the natural heart. Spiritual things are spiritually discerned, and only those who have experienced the new birth can hope to understand it.

The instruction that Christ gave Nicodemus regarding the

process of spiritual rebirth is all that human minds can comprehend. But though man may not understand how the change takes place, God does not leave him ignorant as to what constitutes the transformation.

If after Adam's fall God could have given him the power to obey in the future, then Christ need not have humiliated Himself by taking man's nature and dying on the cross. But because Satan controlled man, Adam had nothing in his heart that would have responded to God's offer of pardon. Man had transferred his love and loyalty to the being who promised to make him a god on earth. Satan caused Adam to look upon God as a stern, unreasonable tyrant, seeking His own selfish interests. The devil still clothes God with his own attributes, causing man to look upon Him with fear and dread. Even the people of God often have mistaken ideas of God's true character, and they find it difficult to trust Him fully.

From eternity God had a plan by which He could unmask the deceiver and demonstrate his character to man. From eternity God knew of the fall of man. He loved him and longed for his salvation. The new birth is a vital part of the plan.

Because so many Christians have confused ideas about the new birth, they have little victory in overcoming Satan's temptations.

"Ye must be born again." "Ye must have a new heart." These expressions and their relationship to the plan of salvation are too little comprehended. Many ministers and religious leaders have presented erroneous doctrines about the change that takes place at conversion. Those converted wait for the peculiar change they believe will take place then. When nothing happens, they lose faith or think that God has rejected them. They do not realize that God has actually accepted them.

159

"For God so loved the world, that he gave his only begotten Son, that whosoever believeth in him should not perish, but have everlasting life," Christ said to Nicodemus. (John 3:16.) Many people can repeat the statement from memory, but unfortunately not every Christian has grasped its full significance and found himself able to believe it, making it an abiding principle in his life. Many believe *about* Christ, but they do not believe *in* Him. They search themselves to see if a "peculiar change" has taken place. Seeing nothing but their usual failures and miserable characters, they doubt the Word of God.

When Nicodemus viewed Jesus hanging on the cross, condemned to die, his heart was broken. As he reflected on the day's scenes, he knew that his sins, his vile, corrupt nature, had caused the Son of God to suffer anguish and agony. He knew that Jesus suffered the punishment he deserved so that he could be free from the condemnation of God's law. The proud Pharisee acknowledged his sinfulness. He knew of Christ's perfect life, and he longed for that righteousness which he himself could not obtain.

As the Holy Spirit wooed him, he responded to the power of that love that drew him nearer and nearer to Christ. He accepted Christ's perfect life of obedience in exchange for his own. The Jewish leader and member of the Sanhedrin knew that God had forgiven his sins because He looked at and judged Christ's life record, not that of Nicodemus.

The Apostle Paul, seeking the spiritual purity and righteousness he could not attain alone, cried out, "O wretched man that I am! who shall deliver me from the body of this death?" Romans 7:24. This cry has gone up from every land, and there is only one answer: "Behold the Lamb of God, which taketh away the sin of the world." Through the simple act of beholding and believing, the Christian allows the Holy Spirit to fashion a new character within him.

Satan constantly endeavors to make man believe that his sins are too great for God to pardon. But God will forgive any sin, no matter how terrible, if the sinner will accept Christ's merit. Just as soon as he responds to the invitation to do so, he has a Substitute. Christ's character stands in place of his character. God sees him as righteous and holy. When a person accepts Christ as his personal Saviour, his Substitute, he is born again.

But this is not to say that the individual never changes. Nicodemus, for example, was a proud individual, self-satisfied. Yet he became humble, painfully aware of his defects of character. The believer finds that where he was formerly despairing and discouraged, he now is joyous in the hope offered to him. He finds that he is capable of accepting such hope, and in his heart he feels deep peace. Before, he doubted, but now he is confident and trusting.

The Christian commits a grave error when he looks upon his sinful condition, constantly talks about it, and regrets his spiritual wretchedness, allowing all this to accumulate. Instead, let him trust in Christ's promise to compensate for his faults and sins, for no amount of sorrow over misconduct will ever give any relief.

John Wesley felt great joy when he learned that he need not spend more years of wearisome and comfortless striving to secure God's favor. Eagerly he renounced all dependence on his own good deeds to earn salvation. He saw that his best endeavors were worthless. God gave as a gift the reconciliation which he had toiled to win by prayers and self-denial and deeds of charity. Like Nicodemus, he bowed in grateful repentance before Christ. Wesley continued a life of denial, no longer in order to gain salvation, but because salvation had come to him without price.

The new birth, which is spiritual, now will become physical reality when Christ returns to earth and transforms the bodies of the redeemed. He who accepts Christ as his personal Substitute is truly a new being, for he has partaken of the divine nature. He has a new mind, new motives and desires. What results from faith in Christ is as certain as if it were already a fact, though the warfare against Satan has not yet ended.

The law of God now written in the heart by faith will then be indelibly imprinted in the inmost being. Man will have no corrupt propensities, no tendencies to fight against, no bent or bias to evil. He will be amazed and delighted by his glorified new body, for he will then be a new creature in every sense of the word. He truly will have been born again.

# 22

# The Sabbath in the Atonement

"REMEMBER the sabbath day, to keep it holy. Six days shalt thou labour and do all thy work: but the seventh day is the sabbath of the Lord thy God: in it thou shalt not do any work, thou, nor thy son, nor thy daughter, thy manservant, nor thy maidservant, nor thy cattle, nor thy stranger that is within thy gates: for in six days the Lord made heaven and earth, the sea, and all that in them is, and rested the seventh day: wherefore the Lord blessed the sabbath day, and hallowed it." Exodus 20:8-11.

Modern Christians need to understand the continuing claims of the moral law, and, understanding it, they will find that the seventh-day Sabbath of the Decalogue has a special interest for them. But unfortunately the majority of Christians believe that the fourth commandment was part of the ceremonial law, that it was a shadowy type which passed away when Christ died.

No Scriptural evidence exists for the assumption, yet theologians offer many arguments in its support. The study of type and antitype will help settle the question.

Type (symbol), which is pictured or enacted prophecy, must continue until it meets its antitype (fulfillment). The shadow must stem from the substance. Human priests continued until the divine Priest came. The earthly sanctuary functioned until the heavenly sanctuary went into operation. Sacrificial animals were used until the Lamb of God died on the altar of Calvary. The three annual feasts held great significance until the gospel dispensation began to fulfill all the inherent prophetic symbolism of Passover, Pentecost, and the Feast of Tabernacles.

In comparing the gospel dispensation with the patriarchal and Levitical periods, one sees that all Biblical symbolism has its fulfillment in a specific *time* that Christ was to perform a certain mission, or in a specific *event.* The ceremonial sabbaths were distinct and separate from the weekly one. Prophetical, they pointed to certain times in the gospel dispensation when special events would take place.

The first ceremonial sabbath in the seven-day Passover festival reached its antitype when Christ rested in the tomb from His role as man's Saviour. The Jews celebrated it the day after they slew the Passover lamb, and it could fall on any day of the week. Jesus was slain on Passover day and rested the next day in the tomb on Passover Sabbath, as predicted.

Unlike the ceremonial sabbaths, the weekly Sabbath did not have its inception at the time Israel became a nation. Rather, man received it in the Garden of Eden as a memorial of creation. God could have created the world in one day or ten days, but He chose the number seven to signify perfection or completeness. God asked man to number the days by sevens to prevent him from forgetting the Creator, who made heaven and earth in six days and rested on the seventh day.

The year Christ died, the ceremonial sabbath of Passover coincided with the weekly Sabbath of creation. The Hebrews termed such an occurrence a "high day," for it was sacred in a double sense. On this particular high day, type met antitype, reality canceled out symbol. Prophecy saw its fulfillment. The Passover sabbath would never again have any significance, for Christ's mission on earth had ended. Christ had made the sacrifice, once for all time. But the weekly Sabbath continued in all its original force. Indeed, Christ had died as man's Substitute to show that the moral law was immutable, that nothing could change it, that the Saviour had come not to abolish it, but to fulfill it. Through all time and all eternity, the Sabbath would remain the sign of God's supreme authority, the indication of His right to be reverenced and worshiped as the Creator.

Christ had no intention of changing the Sabbath given in the fourth commandment. He did not come to earth to weaken or abolish the law of God in any particular. Christ came to express in His own being the love of God. He came to vindicate every precept of the holy law.

Instead of nullifying the law to meet man in his degraded condition, Christ maintained its sacred dignity. The Lord has never saved the sinner by doing away with His law, the foundation of His government in heaven and on earth. God is a Judge, the Guardian of justice. The transgression of His law in even the smallest aspect is sin. The moral excellence of the law must be preserved and vindicated before the universe.

The movements of the earth and the moon determine the length of the month and number of days in the year. But no such natural or scientific basis exists for the length of the week. Only the Bible gives an adequate and authentic explanation for the week's seven-day period of time. Since God gave the Sabbath to man before his fall, it was not part of the prophetic ceremonial law. It is no more reasonable to assume that the fourth commandment was symbolic than to say that the seventh commandment existed for the Jews alone. Both are essential components of the great law of the universe, which says, "Thou shalt love the Lord thy God with all thy heart, . . . and thy neighbour as thyself." Luke 10:27.

165

Jesus said, "The sabbath was made for man [all men], and not man for the sabbath." Mark 2:27. Man came first, and God established the special day of rest and worship for his benefit and happiness. Had he always remained faithful in its observance, there would not now be an atheist or unbeliever in the world. In contemplating the works of nature on the Sabbath, men would have remembered the Creator.

The Sabbath has a special significance for fallen man. God can not only create worlds; He can re-create people's lives and characters. He who said, "Let there be light," also has authority to say, "Thy sins be forgiven thee." "Go, and sin no more."

"Moreover also I gave them my sabbaths, *to be* a sign between me and them, that they might know that I am the Lord that sanctify them." "And hallow my sabbaths; and they shall be a sign between me and you, that ye may know that I am the Lord your God." Ezekiel 20:12, 20.

It is obvious, then, that for us to observe the seventh-day Sabbath we must have accepted the work of atonement and believe in Jesus as our Substitute before God, realizing that our own attempts at righteousness have no value and that Christ's life alone is sufficient to meet the demands of the law. The Christian, then, ceases from his works as God ceased from His. It is not enough, however, that he refrain from physical labor only. The Jewish people were rigorous and exacting in doing so, but they failed to enter into the more important rest of faith mentioned in the fourth chapter of Hebrews. They failed to cease from their own attempts to gain righteousness, their own efforts to fulfill the demands of the law. By trying to earn their own salvation, they failed to accept the merits of Christ's life, death, and mediation in their behalf.

Though Israel was careful and exact in outwardly observing the Sabbath, they did not as a nation enter into its true meaning. They worshiped the Sabbath, but not the Lord of the Sabbath. The Christian church, the modern counterpart of Israel, as a whole has made an equally grave mistake. They accept the Lord of the Sabbath, but reject the Sabbath of the Lord. Since God has designated the seventh day as the sign of His authority, anyone who spurns His command to honor the Sabbath virtually rejects His leadership. Those who profess to follow Christ cannot enter into the rest of faith (Hebrews 4:9) while willfully breaking the Sabbath, for to reject one is to reject the other.

Not all of Israel lost the true meaning of the Sabbath. A faithful minority not only entered into the literal Canaan, but they will also have the joy of seeing their Redeemer in the heavenly Canaan. They entered into the "rest" God promised them. But as not all of literal Israel accepted God's promise of rest, so have many of spiritual Israel failed to grasp the true significance of ceasing from one's own works and entering into the rest of faith. The Hebrews had to learn that they could not conquer Canaan by themselves, but that God would defeat their enemies and allow them to occupy it. The Christian has to learn that he cannot alone conquer Satan and sin. Christ will do it for him.

To those who profess to follow Christ's teachings, the Apostle Paul warns, "Let us therefore fear, lest, a promise being left us of entering into his rest, any of you should seem to come short of it. For unto us was the gospel preached, as well as unto them [Israel]: but the word preached did not profit them, not being mixed with faith in them that heard it. For we which have believed do enter into rest, as he said, As I have sworn in my wrath, if they shall enter into my rest: although the works were finished from the foundation of the world. For he spake in a certain place of the seventh day on this wise, And God did rest the seventh day from all his works. And in this place again, If they shall enter into my rest. Seeing therefore it remaineth that some must enter therein, and they to whom it was first preached entered not in because of unbelief. . . . There remaineth therefore a rest to the people of God." Hebrews 4:1-9.

Those who will honor the Sabbath will indeed find it to be a day of joy and delight. To them God gave the promise, "If thou turn away thy foot from the sabbath, from doing thy pleasure on my holy day; and call the sabbath a delight, the holy of the Lord, honourable, and shalt honour him, not doing thine own ways, nor finding thine own pleasure, nor speaking thine own words: then shalt thou delight thyself in the Lord; and I will cause thee to ride upon the high places of the earth, and feed thee with the heritage of Jacob thy father: for the mouth of the Lord hath spoken it." Isaiah 58:13, 14.

What do the various faiths have to say about Sabbath observance, particularly the shift from worshiping on the seventh day to worshiping on the first day of the week?

The Catholic Church by its own admission boasts of having changed the law of God. *The Catholic World* (Vol. 58, p. 809, March, 1894) declares, "She [the Catholic Church] took the pagan Sunday, and made it the Christian Sunday. . . . The Sun was the foremost god with heathendom. Balder the beautiful, the White God, the old Scandinavians called him. . . . Thus the pagan Sunday, dedicated to Balder, became the Christian Sunday."

And *The Catholic Mirror* (Baltimore, September 23, 1893) states, "The Catholic Church for over one thousand years before the existence of a Protestant, by virtue of her divine mission, *changed the day from Saturday to Sunday. . . . The Christian Sabbath is therefore to this day the acknowl-*

*edged offspring of the Catholic Church* as spouse of the Holy Ghost, without a word of remonstrance from the Protestant world." (Italics supplied.)

W. Long in the *Catholic Press,* Sydney, Australia, August 25, 1900, wrote, "What right, anyhow, have those gentlemen as Protestants to lay down the law as to what is to be done, or not done, on Sunday? *Sunday is a Catholic institution,* and its claim to observance can be defended only on Catholic principles. If 'the Bible, and the Bible alone' is the religion of Protestants, if whatever is not read therein, nor may be proved, thereby has no claim on their faith or observance, what scrap *of title* can they show for all their dogmatic insistence as to the requirements of the Lord's day? From beginning to end of Scripture, there is not a *single passage* that warrants the transfer of weekly public worship from the last day of the week to the first. *Thus Sunday observance is an incongruous adjunct of the Protestant faith and utterly out of keeping with its fundamental principles.* Under the Catholic Church the Sunday supplanted the Jewish Sabbath."

*Clifton Tracts,* Volume 4, page 15, in an article titled "A Question for All Bible Christians," comments, "We Catholics, then, have precisely the same authority for keeping Sunday holy, instead of Saturday, as we have for every other article of our creed; namely, the authority of '*the church of the living God,* the pillar and ground of the truth' [1 Timothy 3:15]; whereas, you who are Protestants have really *no authority for it whatever;* for there is no authority for it in the Bible, and you will not allow that there can be authority for it anywhere else. *Both you and we do, in fact, follow tradition in this matter.*" (Italics supplied.)

Protestant denominations also have much to say on the subject.

169

*Baptist*

"There was and is a commandment to keep holy the Sabbath day, but that Sabbath day was *not Sunday.* It will be said, however, and with some show of triumph, that the Sabbath was transferred from the seventh to the first day of the week, with all its duties, privileges, and sanctions. Earnestly desiring information on this subject, which I have studied for many years, I ask, Where can the record of such a transaction be found? *Not in the New Testament,* absolutely not. There is no Scriptural evidence of the change of the Sabbath institution from the seventh to the first day of the week.

"I wish to say that this Sabbath question, in this aspect of it, is the gravest and most perplexing question connected with Christian institutions which at present claims attention from Christian people; and the only reason that it is not a more disturbing element in Christian thought and in religious discussions, is because the Christian world has settled down content on the conviction that somehow a transference has taken place at the beginning of Christian history. . . .

"To me it seems unaccountable that Jesus, during three years' intercourse with his disciples, often conversing with them upon the Sabbath question, discussing it in some of its various aspects, freeing it from its false glosses, *never alluded to any transference of the day;* also, that during forty days of his resurrection life, *no such thing was intimated.* Nor, so far as we know, did the Spirit, which was given to bring to their remembrance all things whatsoever that he had said unto them, deal with this question. Nor yet did the inspired apostles, in preaching the gospel, founding churches, counseling and instructing those founded, discuss or approach this subject.

"Of course, I quite well know that Sunday did come into use in early Christian history as a religious day, as we learn from the Christian Fathers and other sources. But what a pity that it comes branded with the *mark of paganism,* and christened with the *name of the sun god,* when adopted and sanctioned by *the papal apostasy,* and bequeathed as a sacred legacy to Protestantism!"—Dr. Edward T. Hiscox, author of *The Baptist Manual,* in a paper read before a New York Ministers' Conference, on November 13, 1893, and reported in the New York *Examiner* of November 16, 1893. (Italics supplied.)

*Christian*

" 'But,' say some, 'it was *changed* from the seventh to the first day.' Where? when? and by whom? No man can tell. No, it never was changed, nor could it be, unless creation was to be gone through again: for the reason assigned must be changed before the observance, or respect to the reason, can be changed!! It is all old wives' fables to talk of *the change of the sabbath* from the seventh to the first day. If it be changed, it was that august personage changed it who changes times and laws *ex officio*—I think his name is DOCTOR ANTI-CHRIST."—Alexander Campbell, in *The Christian Baptist,* February 2, 1824.

*Church of England*

"The Sabbath is Saturday, the seventh day of the week.

"The Christian church made no formal, but a gradual and almost unconscious transference of the one day to the other."
—Archdeacon Farrar, quoted in *The Voice From Sinai,* pp. 163, 167.

*Congregationalist*

"The current notion that Christ and His apostles authoritatively substituted the first day for the seventh, is absolutely without any authority in the New Testament."—Dr. Lyman Abbott, in *Christian Union.*

171

### International Sunday School Notes

"Observe the New Testament nowhere treats any part of the law as abolished or repealed. The popular idea that it repeals the Jewish Sabbath and re-enacts a new one has *no warrant* in Scripture. There is no repealing clause in the New Testament; and nothing in it to set aside the Old Testament, or any part of it, as obsolete, common, old-fashioned and useless."—*Peloubet's Select Notes* on the International Sunday School Lessons, 1887.

### Methodist

"The Sabbath was made for man, not for the Jew only, but for man *as man,* for generic, universal man; for man at *all times,* in all places under all circumstances, for the Gentile as well as for the Jew, for the Christian Dispensation as well as for patriarchal and Levitical. It is not a local, not a dispensational thing, but a thing co-existent and *co-extensive with man himself.*"—*Methodist Conference Proceedings,* p. 197, 1881.

### Methodist Episcopal

"It is true, there is *no positive command* for infant baptism. . . . Nor is there any for keeping holy the *first day* of the week."—*Methodist Episcopal Theological Compendium,* pp. 180, 181.

### Protestant Episcopal

"Is there any command in the New Testament to change the day of weekly rest from Saturday to Sunday?—None."—*Manual of Christian Doctrine,* p. 127.

### John Wesley, founder of the Methodist Movement

" 'Remember the Sabbath day to keep it holy; six days shalt thou labour and do all thy work, but the seventh day is the Sabbath of the Lord thy God!'

"It is not thine but God's day. He claims it for His own. He always did claim it for His own, even from the beginning of the world. In six days the Lord made heaven and earth, and rested the seventh day; therefore the Lord blessed the seventh day, and hallowed it. He hallowed it; that is, He made it holy; He reserved it to His own service; He appointed that as long as the sun or moon, the heavens or the earth should endure, the children of men should spend this day in the worship of Him who gave them life and breath and all things."—John Wesley's *Works,* Vol. 6, pp. 352, 353.

Since the beginning in 1844 of the investigative judgment prophesied by Daniel (see chapter 24), the Sabbath has truly become a test to the Christian world. The same Biblical study that brought an understanding of the ministration of Christ in the most holy place of the sanctuary in heaven also brought to view the fourth commandment. John the revelator, in vision, looked into the inner chamber of the sanctuary in heaven and saw "the ark of the testament" which contains the original transcript of the law God delivered to Moses on two tables of stone.

What is in type must be in antitype.

The ark of the testament in the sanctuary on earth contained the two tables written by the finger of God. The entire sanctuary service revolved around the Decalogue, which demanded the life of the transgressor.

So it is in heaven. The entire service of atonement in the gospel dispensation centers around the sacred law before which all men find themselves guilty. It is at the mercy seat that man's Priest and Advocate symbolically sprinkles the blood of His atoning sacrifice over the tables of the testimony which contain not nine commandments, but ten.

John the revelator prophesied of a restoration of the Sabbath doctrine to spiritual Israel. Said he, "I saw another angel ascending from the east, having the seal of the living God." Revelation 7:2. One finds the seal, the mark of God's authority, permanently impressed in the fourth commandment of the Decalogue, where He plainly designates the Sabbath as the sign of His creative power. (See Exodus 20:11.)

As the people of God understand the principles of the sanctuary service in heaven, they realize that they can no longer disregard the express will of the Creator with a clear conscience. Now they must choose between popular custom and tradition, and the direct command of God.

They regard Sunday-keeping as representing an authority to whom they can no longer render homage. In symbolic language the prophet John showed that there would be a minority who would choose a "Thus saith the Lord" even though it meant derision, persecution, or even death itself.

True observance of the Sabbath is the sign of loyalty to God. All who sin ignorantly have a special atonement, but Heaven removes from the book of life the names of those who continue to sin, contrary to what they know. "And whosoever was not found written in the book of life was cast into the lake of fire," we are told in Revelation 20:15. Inclusion in the book of life depends upon a person's reconciliation with God.

Although his best efforts cannot meet the claims of God's holy law, man does not have license to trample upon His requirements. God requires the believer to render his best service, however imperfect that service may be. Then He makes up for the deficiency with His own merit. By his efforts to keep the law, the Christian demonstrates his faith in God's plan for the universe. Also it shows his love for his Creator and Redeemer.

Finally, when Christ returns to the earth, the Sabbath will take on additional significance. "For as the new heavens and the new earth, which I will make, shall remain before me, saith the Lord, so shall your seed and your name remain. And it shall come to pass, that from one new moon to another, and from one sabbath to another, shall all flesh come to worship before me, saith the Lord." Isaiah 66:22, 23.

# Sanctification

IN MUCH the same manner that confusion has built up over the seventh-day Sabbath, misunderstanding surrounds the terms *justification and sanctification, imputed and imparted righteousness.* Too many have only a vague idea of what they mean.

The Christian must not let technical terms upset or confuse him. Faith is simplicity itself, and he who accepts Christ as his personal Saviour need not worry about the small differences in the definitions of such closely related Bible doctrines. It is neither necessary nor wise to attempt to draw a fine line of distinction between them.

The story of the thief on the cross who accepted Jesus provides a good illustration of what happens in the life of each person who believes the gospel. The thief saw himself utterly lost and condemned to death. He knew that he had no hope of reprieve. He could not do a thing to save himself.

As soon as his eyes fell on Jesus, he recognized Christ to be a man completely unlike himself. He had heard of Jesus' unreproachable life, of how He went about doing good, living only to bless others. He had heard His pleading request when the soldiers drove the nails into His hands, "Father, forgive them; for they know not what they do." Why should Christ hang there naked like himself, bruised and bleeding? the thief wondered. Why was He beaten, spat upon, mocked and insulted? Why the crown of thorns on His head? The thief conceded the justice of his own sentence, but what had this Man done?

The Holy Spirit influenced the thief's heart. He saw that Jesus was dying for his own life of crime, so that he might stand guiltless in the judgment which still awaited him. The significance of what Christ was doing overwhelmed him, broke his heart. Humbly he confessed his great need and helplessness. Gratefully he accepted Christ's gift of pardon before the law of God and the promise of eternal life.

The moment the thief repented, he received all that Jesus could possibly give—justification, sanctification, and righteousness. He would share Christ's divine nature, which would enable him to stand before the heavenly tribunal and meet the highest demands of the law.

Christ's death justified the thief and declared him "not guilty." Jesus had taken his sins, and he was free. But the law demands more than that of anyone wanting to enter heaven. Heaven demands a perfect character, not merely freedom from sin. No man is born with character. It is something that each person must develop during a probationary period before Christ's second coming. He must withstand trials to see if he will trust God supremely, or if he will give his allegiance to Satan. The law requires perfection of character, something the thief did not have. But Jesus was his Substitute, and now the Saviour's character would stand in place of his. The law had nothing more to require.

Christ's death justified the thief, and the Holy Spirit, working on his heart, sanctified him. Through Jesus, he now had a holy character, and the law had nothing more to require. The Father loved him for accepting the gift of His Son during a time when almost everyone else cursed and reviled Christ.

Listing the various kinds of people that will not reach

177

heaven, the Apostle Paul adds, "And such were some of you: but ye are washed, but ye are sanctified, but ye are justified in the name of the Lord Jesus, and by the Spirit of our God." 1 Corinthians 6:11. "But of him are ye in Christ Jesus, who of God is made unto us wisdom, and righteousness, and sanctification, and redemption," he states elsewhere. (1 Corinthians 1:30.)

When he accepted Jesus, the thief received both his title to and his qualification for heaven. Because he felt and recognized his own spiritual poverty and weakness, he could receive the gift which God offered him. It freed him from the defilement of sin. But the Christian must never make the mistake that once saved he is always saved. The Christian life has just begun. The enemy of God will do all in his power to wrest eternal life from man. He will use every inducement, every artifice conceivable, to lead man to regard Christ's gift lightly. The devil is an expert in appealing to men's minds. He uses the power he employed to secure the fall of Adam and Eve to entice believers back into the slavery of sin. He knows that as long as man beholds Christ with the eye of faith, he can have no power over him. Every Christian must realize that the time will never come in his life when Satan's shadow will not cross his path as the evil one endeavors to obstruct faith. The Christian's faith must cut through the shadow. Only he who clings to his faith until the end will be finally saved.

The Christian has a growing knowledge of the plan of salvation. He understands and appreciates Christ more every day. The new understanding creates in the believer's heart a hatred for sin. Without Christ's converting and spiritually renewing power, man would still be Satan's captive, a servant ready to do his bidding.

But the new principle in the soul creates conflict where

178

peace had existed before. The power which Christ implants enables man to resist the tyrant and usurper. Whoever abhors sin instead of entertaining a love for it, whoever resists and conquers the passions that formerly held sway, displays the operation of a principle wholly divine.

One of the most subtle deceptions that Satan has for distracting Christians is to lead them to think that once they are pardoned and justified, the work of sanctification is up to them. It is the individual's responsibility, he implies, to go on to perfection, to climb upward to the gates of heaven. He further leads men to believe that "climbing" means gaining in moral achievements, giving up bad habits, renouncing the world's pleasures.

Satan wants man to think that sanctification consists of such things as practicing the Golden Rule, performing various acts of worship, and denying oneself certain harmful indulgences. As the Christian seeks to obey the law of God and to follow the rules and regulations laid down by the church, all of which he should indeed do, he comes to believe that Christ is imparting His righteousness to him bit by bit so that it becomes in fact his own. He becomes "puffed up," feeling he is better than others. He believes that through his own efforts he will eventually become a fit candidate for heaven. "Help me to become worthy" is his fervent prayer.

But Jesus is, and always will be, man's only worthiness. Man's spiritual condition throughout his life is worthless, as the Bible phrases it, like "filthy rags." (Isaiah 64:6.) It is Christ's righteousness which entitles a person to Heaven's blessings. But the Christian does not receive them simply because he has entertained the notion that he could do anything himself to merit them.

Man must give up such an idea. A sin of the most subtle

179

sort, it leads to self-dependence and pride, no matter how sincere the motives. The idea that one can somehow become worthy of God's blessings appeals to man's pride, but until he learns that he can do nothing to commend himself to God, he will never enter heaven. He can do absolutely nothing to gain divine favor.

Some conscientious individuals divide their trust, keeping it partly in God and partly in themselves. Instead of trusting Christ to make them completely acceptable before God, they depend upon watchfulness against temptation and the performance of certain duties for His approval. But such a faith is also worthless.

Though Christians readily accept the Bible truth that justification comes only through faith, many have been led to believe that sanctification results from personal activities. But the only works that have any value with God are those initiated by faith. The Jewish people once asked Christ, "What shall we do, that we might work the works of God?" "This is the work of God, *that ye believe on him whom he hath sent,*" He answered. (John 6:28, 29.)

Justification and sanctification may be compared to an ideal marriage relationship, justification being the wedding ceremony, which unites the betrothed, and sanctification being their life together, their daily relationship. Love, understanding, and trust deepen as time goes on. When one or the other makes a mistake or falls short of perfection, it does not break the relationship. Nor do the couple have to daily repeat the marriage vows, because in the true love relationship, the man and woman unconsciously live them out in their lives. One delights to please the other.

It is thus with the Christian's relationship with Christ. By daily beholding Him with the eye of faith, his love deepens and grows until it becomes his greatest pleasure to do Christ's will. Sanctification involves maintaining the experience of justification, the act of daily having Christ assume responsibility for one's sins and accepting His obedience in place of personal shortcomings. It is the relationship we maintain with Christ by living at the foot of the cross. There Christ is our victory.

Because man possesses a sinful, rebellious nature, he will never become less and less sinful in his mortal life, and more and more righteous. He is forever erring. All are helpless, condemned sinners, even as was the thief on the cross. But the Christian has the privilege of knowing Jesus better and better, and of having his faith grow stronger and stronger. Good works will then appear in his life as an indication of the faith he possesses, and he will reflect Christ's character in all his activities. But if such good works fail to appear, it is evidence that faith is dead.

It has been previously pointed out that good works will not save one person, as John Wesley discovered; yet it is equally impossible to be saved without them. Each believer must have a sincere desire to obey the will of God. When he exerts an effort toward such an end, Christ accepts it as adequate, making up for the deficiency with His own perfection. God has provided a salvation so complete that mankind's best deeds can add nothing to it. The Christian needs daily conversion, for as long as Satan reigns, he will encounter a strong undercurrent of evil. He must receive divine strength moment by moment, or he will find it impossible to remain converted. The struggle for conquest over self is a lifelong one.

Paul knew this when he said, "I die daily." 1 Corinthians 15:31. He saw to it that he did not follow his own desires, but the will of God, even though he might find it unpleasant to his own nature. Sanctification is a continuing process.

Growth in grace is not easy. It means increasing one's knowledge of the plan of salvation and knowing Jesus better every day. Grace creates in the believer's heart a hatred for sin. Without the converting and renewing power of grace, man would still be Satan's captive, a servant ready to do his bidding.

Though good works certainly should appear in the believer's life, to equate sanctification with moral development is to make a serious mistake. Many in the world who make no claim to be Christians would never stoop to commit an immoral act or tell an untruth. Taught from childhood to value integrity for its own worth, they are upright, law-abiding citizens. But the morality of the world is valueless in the sight of Heaven, for it is tainted with selfishness and leads its possessor to feel spiritually in need of nothing. Such men and women testify to the world that man need not accept Christ in order to become "good," for are they not much better than some professed Christians?

Regrettably, Satan often has his greatest success through people who least suspect that they are under his control. Many cultured, intelligent people would never commit an immoral act, yet they are Satan's most influential agents. They present one of the greatest threats to Christianity.

Heaven pronounces perfect the drunkard on Skid Row who acknowledges his helplessness and accepts Christ, but the fine law-abiding person of refinement who refuses to acknowledge his need of a Substitute will find no place in the heavenly kingdom. Such a "polished instrument in the hands of Satan" may be a respected church member, admired as a paragon of virtue, but his profession of faith renders him more guilty than he would be were he an open enemy of God. Many have pointed out that the strongest bastion of vice in the world is not the undesirable life of the abandoned sinner or degraded outcast, but a life which appears virtuous, honorable, noble, while at the same time indulging in even a single vice. To the individual secretly, silently struggling against some giant temptation, such an example will be one of the most powerful enticements to sin. Genius, talent, sympathy, even generous and kindly deeds, may become Satan's decoys.

To feel that overcoming bad habits offers evidence of sanctification is to confuse the issue. Unless Christ's merit validates such improvements, they have no value. They represent only a moral achievement. On the other hand, the believer who struggles faithfully against inherited or cultivated propensities to evil may claim victory. He has acknowledged his need and laid his sins on Jesus. Heaven accepts Christ's obedience in place of man's failure. Though he errs, he does not sin willfully. He hates the sin that caused the Saviour so much agony, and he turns from it with loathing. His love deepens as he sees how much his salvation cost. It is a love which becomes a living, acting principle, entering into all of his activities. Every talent, every capability, he develops and trains for God's service.

Never get the notion that it is enough to *say* that one is a helpless, condemned sinner. The Christian has to feel it in his very being. It is possible to be proud of one's own humility. Such a person must rid himself of pride and self-sufficiency. Of all sins, pride is the most hopeless, the most difficult to overcome. Thus only as the believer beholds Christ does he develop a true understanding of himself.

Some claim that they are covered with Christ's righteousness when actually they have no connection at all with Christ. If they cherish even one sin, it is enough to nullify the power of the gospel.

183

Perfect sanctification is perfect love. It leads the Christian to love both God and man. As he becomes aware of his own unworthiness, pride can no longer exist within him. Only beholding Christ will produce such a love. Without Christ, man can do nothing that is not polluted with selfishness. God finds acceptable only that which man does through the inspiration of faith. Sanctification is not a gradual elimination of the sinful nature. It is seeking to gain heaven through the merits of Christ while doing one's best to obey His will. To know God's will and to know what constitutes Christ's merits require careful study into the plan of salvation, and into the law of God. To forgo such study will cause faith to grow cold. Self-righteousness will take the place of dependence on Christ, and doubt and unbelief will replace the former religious experience.

# 24

# The Atonement Prophecy

"UNTO two thousand and three hundred days; then shall the sanctuary be cleansed." Daniel 8:14. These momentous words form the core of a vision of the atonement received by the prophet Daniel. The Bible student will recognize these words as referring to the Hebrew sanctuary's Day of Atonement, or "expiation day," the day the sanctuary was cleansed of the confessed sins that had accumulated during the year.

But the question arises, What sanctuary would be cleansed at the end of the 2300 days? Daniel 8:10 states, "And it waxed great, even to the host of heaven; and it cast down some of the host and of the stars to the ground, and stamped upon them." The previous verse mentions a power symbolized by the phrase "a little horn," with its eventual influence and tragic effect even upon "the host of heaven," doubtless referring to God's people.

Further growth of the antagonistic and oppressive power appears in verse 11: "Yea, he magnified himself even to the prince of the host, and by him the daily sacrifice was taken away, and the place of his sanctuary was cast down." The *prince of the host* must be Christ. The twelfth verse depicts further desecration of religious truth, with a subsequent growth and prosperity of the little horn: "And an host was given him against the daily sacrifice by reason of transgression, and it cast down the truth to the ground; and it practised, and prospered."

In the midst of such darkness and gloom, Daniel, in his

vision, overheard one saint ask the pleading question, "How long shall be the vision concerning the daily sacrifice, and the transgression of desolation, to give both the sanctuary and the host to be trodden under foot?" Verse 13.

In answer came the mystical reply, "Unto two thousand and three hundred days; then shall the sanctuary be cleansed." Verse 14.

It must be borne in mind that at the time of the writing of the eighth chapter of Daniel no earthly tabernacle service existed. Israel was a captive nation, and its conquerors forbade the tabernacle ritual. The passage could not refer to the Hebrew sanctuary. Neither, it will be recalled, was the Jewish Temple ever cleansed in 2,300 days or 2,300 years, but once a year, on the Day of Atonement.

The Bible mentions only two sanctuaries: the Hebrew, or typical; and the heavenly, or antitypical. Since the tabernacle under discussion cannot be the earthly, it has to be the heavenly, or antitypical, and its cleansing according to the prophecy will be on the great antitypical Day of Atonement.

About 1830 a period of remarkable religious fervor began in various parts of the world. Great interest in the prophecies of Daniel arose among religious leaders of the day. Prominent among these was William Miller, of Low Hampton, New York, whose work met with favor because of his careful and consistent study of the prophecies.

Not long after he started preaching the results of his careful study, a multitude of colaborers joined him and supported his belief about the rapidly approaching conclusion of the gospel age. His followers included men of influence and piety. While Miller was mistaken on a vital point, in principle and a great number of particulars he was right. He was basically correct in his assumptions, and made an immense advance over the theological system of his day.

One of the errors in reasoning by him and his contemporaries resulted from the assumption that the sanctuary referred to in the Book of Daniel was the earth. From this mistaken conception Miller and his associates naturally concluded that the Saviour would return to the earth to cleanse it at the end of the prophetic period of time mentioned in Daniel 8:14. When the date they set for Christ's second coming passed without the Lord's appearance, a number of them reviewed their deductions until they discovered the reason for their error. They realized that the sanctuary in the eighth chapter of Daniel referred to the heavenly and not the earthly. Obviously, then, the sanctuary in connection with the 2300 days also was the heavenly.

Christ would cleanse the heavenly sanctuary, not the earth, at the close of what constitutes the longest time prophecy in the Bible. As the high priest in the typical service entered once a year into the most holy place, so Jesus, at the close of His ministerial role in the first apartment, entered once into the second apartment to cleanse the sanctuary in heaven of the record of sin He had carried in at His ascension forty days after His resurrection.

The process of atonement in the Levitical period covered a full year, ending with the events transpiring on the Day of Atonement. But the sanctuary of the gospel age was to be cleansed after 2300 prophetic days.

Further study and consideration of the time prophecy makes it apparent that the period of 2300 days is prophetic time and not literal. The unit of time measurement is symbolic. The principle given in the Bible for reckoning prophetic time is for a day to equal a year. (See Ezekiel 4:6 and Numbers 14:34.) It is a principle Bible students have recognized throughout the ages. Joachim, Abbot of Calabria, one of the great ecclesiastical figures of the twelfth century, applied the year-day principle to the 1260-day period mentioned several times in the Scriptures. (Revelation 11:3; 12:6.)

"The woman, clothed with the sun, who signifies the church, remained hidden in the wilderness from the face of the serpent, a day without doubt being accepted for a year, and a thousand two hundred and sixty days for the same number of years."—Joachim of Floris, *Concordantia*, Book 2, chap. 16, p. 12b.

The great scientist Sir Isaac Newton, in his memorable book *Observations Upon the Prophecies of Daniel*, Part 1, chapter 8, page 114, states, "Three times and a half; that is, for 1260 solar years, reckoning a time for a calendar year of 360 days, and a day for a solar year. After which the judgment is to sit, and they shall take away his dominion, not at once, but by degrees, to consume, and to destroy it unto the end."

The year-day principle numbers among its supporters such names as Augustine, Tichonius, Primasius, Andreas, the Venerable Bede, Ambrosius, Anspartus, Berengaud, and Bruno Astensis, besides several leading modern expositors. But what is more conclusive is the fact that prophecies have actually been fulfilled according to the principle.

A striking example of the correctness of the year-day principle in calculating Bible prophecy was the prediction regarding the fall of the Ottoman Empire, which many Bible scholars see described in Revelation 9. The empire, composed of all the main Mohammedan tribes, had its capital at Constantinople. For nearly four hundred years it had been a world power, but it crumpled, to almost everyone's surprise, just as Bible prophecy foretold that it would.

Josiah Litch, a prominent minister of the early 1830's,

became interested in Revelation 9, and in 1838 published a paper stating that according to his calculations the Ottoman Empire would fall in 1840, sometime in the month of August. Then in the August 1, 1840, *Signs of the Times,* he wrote, "Allowing the first period, 150 years, to have been exactly fulfilled before Deacozes ascended the throne by permission of the Turks, and that the 391 years, fifteen days, commenced at the close of the first period, it will end on the 11th of August, 1840, when the Ottoman power in Constantinople may be expected to be broken. And this, I believe, will be found to be the case."

The event fulfilled the prediction, when on that date Turkey, through her ambassadors, accepted an ultimatum from the European powers that placed the Islamic empire for all practical purposes under Christian control.

Since the 2300 days of Daniel 8 ended with the commencement of the Day of Atonement, every full year, counting backward, would be a kind of anniversary of the Day of Atonement. Therefore, a strong possibility exists that the decree was also proclaimed 2300 years previously on the Day of Atonement. The passage, "Unto two thousand and three hundred days" contains no mention of fractional years. All are full years. As with any anniversary, the Day of Atonement would be celebrated on the same day yearly for 2300 years, finally ending on the Day of Atonement.

To use an example, the United States celebrated its one hundred and ninety-third year of independence on July 4, 1969. If one subtracts 193 years from 1969, he obtains the date July 4, 1776. Therefore, it is reasonable to believe that July 4, 1776, marked the first Independence Day for the United States of America.

It is similar with the 2300 days of Daniel 8:14. The

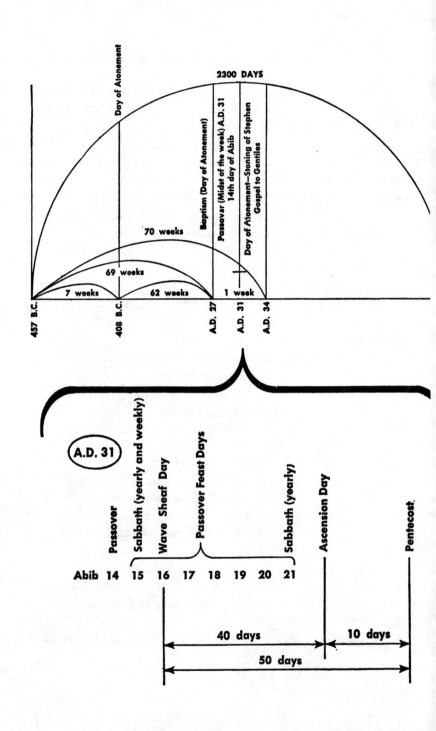

prophecy culminated on the Day of Atonement after 2300 years. The time period, then, for the prophecy began 2300 years before on the same day, the Day of Atonement. Following the line of reasoning, the seventy weeks, the seven weeks, the sixty-nine weeks, and the sixty-two weeks (see Daniel 9) all began and ended with the commencement of the Day of Atonement, for they are full years, beginning and ending on the same day.

Christ became the Messiah at His baptism at the close of the sixty-nine weeks on the Day of Atonement, when He "began to be about thirty years of age." (Luke 3:23.) In the "midst of the week" the Saviour was crucified, causing all the sacrifice and oblation to cease. History confirms the fact that His crucifixion took place on Passover day, six months after the Day of Atonement. He rested in the grave on the Sabbath, the day after Passover, and the first day of the seven-day Passover feast. As predicted by the symbolism of the earthly sanctuary service, He arose on wave-sheaf day, the firstfruits of those who will arise at His triumphant second coming. And even more, Heaven inaugurated Him to His work in the heavenly sanctuary on Pentecost, fifty days after wave-sheaf day.

Like the other symbolic events of the sanctuary service Christ has fulfilled, the symbolism of the Hebrew ritual must be completed at a specific time in earth's history. Daniel has pinpointed the year the prophecy began:

"Know therefore and understand, that from the going forth of the commandment to restore and to build Jerusalem unto the Messiah the Prince shall be seven weeks, and threescore and two weeks: the street shall be built again, and the wall, even in troublous times.

"And after threescore and two weeks shall Messiah be cut

off, but not for himself: and the people of the prince that shall come shall destroy the city and the sanctuary; and the end thereof shall be with a flood, and unto the end of the war desolations are determined.

"And he shall confirm the covenant with many for one week: and in the midst of the week he shall cause the sacrifice and the oblation to cease, and for the overspreading of abominations he shall make it desolate, even until the consumation, and that determined shall be poured upon the desolate." Daniel 9:25-27.

In his brief but explicit statement, the angel gave to Daniel not only the event which marks the beginning of the time prophecy of seventy weeks, but also the events which were to take place at its close. The Bible student has two tests to check the accuracy of the prophecy. In addition, the period of seventy weeks has three further subdivisions which help determine definitely the prophecy's time span. One of the divisions is again divided, and the intermediate events are given to mark the termination of each part. If a date can be found which will harmonize with all the events, it will doubtless be the correct application.

The command to restore and rebuild Jerusalem came in three successive orders. The seventh chapter of Ezra records the last one, given by Artaxerxes in 457 B.C. More complete than the two previous ones, it included not only the rebuilding of the Temple and restoring the Temple worship of the Jews, but the restoration of Israel's civil state and polity.

The decree of Cyrus (Ezra 1:1-4), proclaimed in 536 B.C., pertained to the rebuilding of the Jewish Temple. The decree of Darius (Ezra 6:1-12), made in 519 B.C., reestablished the authority of the first decree.

In addition, there was the commission to Nehemiah from

Artaxerxes in 444 B.C. (Nehemiah 2.) Evidence exists that Nehemiah's commission consisted of little more than permission to travel to Jerusalem. Apparently it was not written, although he did send letters to the governors beyond the Euphrates River and an order to the king's forest for timber.

When Nehemiah arrived in Jerusalem thirteen years after the third decree to Ezra, he found the rulers, priests, nobles, and general population already engaged in the work of rebuilding Jerusalem. (Nehemiah 2:16.) Obviously the work was already well under way, and Nehemiah completed what he came to accomplish in fifty-two days.

From the foregoing information it is not difficult to determine which decree constitutes the true commission to reconstruct Jerusalem. It appears to be that given to Ezra in 457 B.C., because it is the most complete and effective. It extended the Jews' political and civil rights and restored Temple worship. Indeed, Ezra spoke of the three decrees as being one. "They builded, and finished it, according to the commandment of the God of Israel, and according to the commandment of Cyrus, and Darius, and Artaxerxes king of Persia." Ezra 6:14.

The second test of the accuracy of the 457 B.C. date is, of course, to apply it to the subdivisions of the prophecy, several of which contain specific events with well-documented dates.

Forty-nine years were allotted to the rebuilding of the wall. Humphrey Prideaux (*The Old and New Testament Connected in the History of the Jews,* Vol. 1, p. 322) has expressed the following: "In the fifteenth year of Darius Nothus ended the first seven weeks of the seventy weeks of Daniel's prophecy. For then the restoration of the church and state of the Jews in Jerusalem and Judea was fully finished, in that last act of reformation, which is recorded in the thirteenth chapter of

193

Nehemiah, from the twenty-third verse to the end of the chapter, just *forty-nine* years after it had been first begun by Ezra in the seventh year of Artaxerxes Longimanus." (Italics supplied.)

The sixty-nine weeks, or 483 years, would extend to Messiah the Prince. Adding 483 years to the date 457 B.C. brings us to the year A.D. 27. The Gospel writer Luke recorded an event that occurred in A.D. 27 worthy of recognition as a prophetic landmark. "Now when all the people were baptized, it came to pass, that Jesus also being baptized, and praying, the heaven was opened, and the Holy Ghost descended in a bodily shape like a dove upon him, and a voice came from heaven, which said, Thou art my beloved Son; in thee I am well pleased." Luke 3:21, 22.

Mark 1:14, 15 records Christ's words in regard to God's great timetable: "Jesus came . . . preaching the gospel of the kingdom of God, and saying, The time is fulfilled." Doubtless Jesus had reference to the sixty-nine weeks of Daniel, which would bring Him to the time of His public ministry. The Messiah had now come, and with His own lips He announced the termination of another prophetic period.

The seventy weeks (490 years) allotted to Israel came to their conclusion in the autumn of A.D. 34. The date marks the martyrdom of Stephen, the formal rejection of the gospel of Christ by the Jewish Sanhedrin through their act of persecuting the disciples, and the turning of the apostles' attention to evangelizing the Gentiles.

In "the midst of the week" God caused the sacrificial system to cease. The "week" described has reference to the period of seven years between the sixty-ninth week and the seventieth week, or between A.D. 27 and 34. Its "midst" would be three and a half years, or in the spring of A.D. 31. History and the Scriptures agree on the importance of the date—Christ was crucified on Passover day, the fourteenth day of Abib in the spring of A.D. 31.

The decree marking the beginning of the seventy-week prophecy also serves as the starting point for the longer 2300 days of the Book of Daniel. The most far-reaching decree to rebuild Jerusalem was made in 457 B.C. Since the 2300 days ended on the Day of Atonement, the prophecy probably also had its beginning on the Day of Atonement, 457 B.C. Most Bible scholars concur that Ezra's work of reestablishing civil and religious administration in Jerusalem began in the fall of that year because he arrived in Jerusalem in the fifth month. (Ezra 7:9.) He could scarcely have begun much before the seventh month, the time of the Day of Atonement.

The seventy weeks, or 490 years, ended in A.D. 34. Subtracting 490 from 2300 obtains the figure 1810. Adding 1810 to 34 indicates the year 1844 to be the end point of the momentous 2300 days. Comparison of the prophecy to the Hebrew sanctuary ritual leads to the conclusion that the tenth day seventh month of the Jewish calendar—or October 22, 1844, according to the Christian calendar, the Day of Atonement for 1844—represented the close of the prophecy. Type met antitype, fulfillment canceled out symbol, as man's divine Priest ushered in the final Day of Atonement and began the closing aspect of His ministry to redeem the fallen human race.

In unmistakable fashion, the prophecy given in the eighth and ninth chapters of Daniel demonstrated the remarkable way God chose to tell the fallen sons and daughters of Adam, through types and prophecies, the wonders of atonement. The 2300 days fixed the time of the various events culminating in the entrance of Christ into the second apartment of the sanctuary in heaven. The prophecies pointed to the year of fulfillment, while the Hebrew symbolism depicted the day.

The ritual of the Hebrew priest taking the sins of the people from the Temple on a specific day, the Day of Atonement, offered an impressive visual aid to tell about the true or antitypical Day of Atonement. It is a portrayal as valid as when on Passover day, A.D. 31, the great antitypical Passover Lamb was slain for the sins of the world on the same day the Israelites had celebrated their deliverance for 1,500 years.

The antitypical Day of Atonement was ushered in about the middle of the nineteenth century. When will the Majesty of heaven arise and utter the fateful words of never-ending life or death, "It is finished"? "He that is unjust, let him be unjust still: and he which is filthy, let him be filthy still: and he that is righteous, let him be righteous still: and he that is holy, let him be holy still." Revelation 22:11.

The atonement is the golden key that opens the door of eternity to glorious life everlasting with God and Christ and all the heavenly beings.

# APPENDIX

## The Atonement in the Writings of Ellen G. White

*(Italics have been supplied throughout this compilation to enable the eye to catch pertinent points at a glance.)*

### Supplementary Material for Chapter One

"Under the symbol of the king of Tyrus, the Scriptures give us a description of the character and destiny of the first great rebel against the law of God. He who knows the end from the beginning, had His laws and commandments before the world was created; and Satan chose to question His claims before the angels of heaven, because the law set forth the Omnipotent as the only true and living God, and forbade the worship of any other being. . . .

"It is the prerogative of God alone to prescribe the duty of men and angels. . . . The law of God should be obeyed even though there were no authority to enforce it, and no rewards for its obedience. The highest interests of men and angels are conserved in obeying the law of God."—*Signs of the Times,* October 8, 1912.

"He [Lucifer] was not immediately dethroned. . . . Long was he retained in Heaven. *Again and again was he offered pardon on condition of repentance and submission.*"—*The Spirit of Prophecy,* Vol. 4, pp. 319, 320.

"The battle going on in this world was witnessed by the heavenly universe, and by the worlds unfallen. They saw the purposes of hate cherished by the wily foe against the only-begotten Son of God. Satan's enmity against truth and righteousness was seen. By his treatment of Christ, Satan demonstrated the falsity of his own attributes, and of his deceiving, crooked pretensions as the friend of God. He showed himself to be the enemy of God and of man. The sacrificial offering upon the cross of Calvary sounded the death knell of Satan and of all who choose him as their leader. *He fell forever from the sympathy of the heavenly angels.*"—*Signs of the Times,* June 17, 1897.

"The human family have all transgressed the law of God, and as transgressors of the law, *man is hopelessly ruined,* for he is the enemy of God, without strength to do any good thing."—*Ibid.,* June 27, 1911.

"By shedding the blood of the Son of God, he had uprooted himself from the sympathies of the heavenly beings. . . . Whatever attitude he might assume, *he could no longer await the angels as they came from the heavenly courts, and before them accuse Christ's brethren of being clothed with the garments of blackness and the defilement of sin.*"—*The Desire of Ages,* p. 761.

"*The casting down of Satan* as an accuser of the brethren in heaven was accomplished by the great work of Christ in giving up His life. Notwithstanding Satan's persistent opposition, the plan of redemption was being carried out. Man was esteemed of sufficient value for Christ to sacrifice His life for him. Satan, knowing that the empire he had usurped would in the end be wrested from him, determined to spare no pains to destroy as many as possible of the creatures whom God had created in His image."—*Signs of the Times,* April 22, 1913.

"Satan's position in heaven had been next to the Son of God. He was first among the angels. His power had been debasing, but God could not reveal it in its true light and carry all heaven in harmony with Him in removing him with his evil influences. His power was increasing, but the evil was yet unrecognized. *It was a deadly power to the universe, but for the security of the worlds and the government of heaven, it was necessary that it should develop and be revealed in its true light.*

"In carrying out his enmity to Christ until He hung upon the cross of Calvary, with wounded, bruised body and broken heart, *Satan completely uprooted himself from the affections of the universe.* It was then seen that God had in His Son denied Himself, giving Himself for the sins of the world, because He loved mankind."—*Selected Messages,* Book One, pp. 341, 342.

"God bowed His head satisfied. Now justice and mercy could blend. Now He could be just, and yet the Justifier of all who should believe on Christ. He [God] looked upon the victim expiring on the cross, and said, 'It is finished. The human race shall have another trial.' The redemption price was paid, *and Satan fell like lightning from heaven.*"—*The Youth's Instructor,* June 21, 1900. (Quoted in *Questions on Doctrine,* p. 674.)

"All are punished according to their deeds. The sins of the righteous have been transferred to Satan, the originator of evil, who must bear their penalty. Thus he is made to suffer not only for his own rebellion, but for all the sins which he has caused God's people to commit. His punishment is to be far greater than that of those whom he has deceived. After all have perished who fell by his deceptions, he is still to live and suffer on. In the cleansing flames the wicked are at last destroyed, root and branch,—Satan the root, his followers the branches. The justice of God is satisfied, and the saints and all the angelic host say with a loud voice, Amen."—*The Spirit of Prophecy,* Vol. 4, pp. 488, 489.

## Supplementary Material for Chapter Two

"The work of redemption involved consequences of which it is difficult for man to have any conception. . . . To human beings striving for conformity to the divine image, there is to be imparted an outlay of heaven's treasure, an excellency of power, *that will place them higher than even the angels who have never fallen.*"—*Christ's Object Lessons,* p. 163.

"The sin of Adam and Eve caused a fearful separation between God and man, and here Christ steps in between fallen man and God, and says to man, You may yet come to the Father; there is a plan devised through which God can be reconciled to man, and man to God; and through a mediator you can approach God."—*Review and Herald,* May 31, 1870.

"Christ's work was to reconcile man to God through His human nature, and God to man through His divine nature."—*Redemption: or the Temptation of Christ (Life of Christ,* Vol. 1), p. 37.

"In Christ were united the human and the divine. His mission was to reconcile God to man, and man to God. His work was to unite the finite with the Infinite."—*Redemption: or the First Advent of Christ* (*Life of Christ*, Vol. 1), p. 33.

"From everlasting He was the Mediator of the covenant." —*Selected Messages*, Book One, p. 247.

"Adam and Eve were given a probation in which to return to their allegiance; and in this plan of benevolence all their posterity were embraced. After the fall, Christ became Adam's instructor. He acted in God's stead toward humanity, saving the race from immediate death. He took upon Him the work of mediator between God and man. In the fullness of time He was to be revealed in human form. He was to take His position at the head of humanity by taking the nature but not the sinfulness of man. In heaven was heard the voice, 'The Redeemer shall come to Zion, and unto them that turn from transgression in Jacob, saith the Lord.' "—*Signs of the Times*, May 29, 1901.

"The reconciliation of man to God could be accomplished only through a mediator who was equal with God, possessed of attributes that would dignify, and declare him worthy to treat with the Infinite God in man's behalf, and also represent God to a fallen world. Man's substitute and surety must have man's nature, a connection with the human family whom he was to represent, and, as God's ambassador, he must partake of the divine nature, have a connection with the Infinite, in order to manifest God to the world, and be a mediator between God and man."—*Selected Messages*, Book One, p. 257.

"Our dependence is not in what man can do; it is in what God can do for man through Christ. . . . We are not to be anxious about what Christ and God think of us, but about what God thinks of Christ, our Substitute. Ye are accepted in the Beloved."—*Ibid.*, Book Two, pp. 32, 33.

"This Saviour was to be a Mediator, to stand between the Most High and His people. Through this provision, a way was opened whereby the guilty sinner might find access to God through the mediation of another. The sinner could not come in his own person, with his guilt upon him, and with no greater merit than he possessed in himself. Christ alone could open the way."—*Review and Herald*, December 17, 1872. (*Questions on Doctrine*, p. 688.)

## Supplementary Material for Chapter Three

"There is in nature the continual working of the Father and the Son. Said Christ, 'My Father worketh hitherto, and I work.'

"*God has finished His creative work,* but His energy is still exerted in upholding the objects of His creation."—*Bible Echo and Signs of the Times*, January, 1886.

"The work of creation was a manifestation of His love; but *the gift of God to save the guilty and ruined race, alone reveals the infinite depths of divine tenderness and compassion.*"—*Testimonies*, Vol. 5, p. 739.

"The plan for our redemption was not an afterthought, a plan formulated after the fall of Adam. It was a revelation of 'the mystery which hath been kept in silence through times

eternal.' Romans 16:25, R.V. It was an unfolding of the principles that from eternal ages have been the foundation of
God's throne. *From the beginning, God and Christ knew of
the apostasy of Satan, and of the fall of man through the deceptive power of the apostate.* God did not ordain that sin
should exist, but He foresaw its existence, and made provision
to meet the terrible emergency."—*The Desire of Ages,* p. 22.

"God created man for His own glory. *It was His purpose
to repopulate heaven with the human race,* if after test and
trial they proved to be loyal to Him."—*Signs of the Times,*
May 29, 1901.

"How great the love of God is! God made the world to
enlarge heaven. He desired a larger family. And before man
was created, God and Christ entered into a covenant that if he
fell from his allegiance, Christ would bear the penalty of
transgression."—*Review and Herald,* June 25, 1908.

"God, in counsel with His Son, formed the plan of creating
man in His own image. Man was to be placed upon probation.
He was to be tested and proved. If he should bear the test of
God, and remain loyal and true through the first trial, he was
not to be beset with continual temptations, but was to be ex-
alted equal with the angels, and made, thenceforth, immortal."
—*Redemption: or the Temptation of Christ (Life of Christ,*
Vol. 1), p. 6.

"By giving His life for the life of the world, Christ bridged
the gulf that sin had made, joining this sin-cursed earth to the
universe of heaven as a province. *God chose this world to be
the theater of His mighty work of grace.*"—*Signs of the Times,*
February 22, 1899.

"*We were brought into existence because we were needed.* How sad the thought that if we stand on the wrong side, in the ranks of the enemy, we are lost to the design of our creation. We are disappointing our Redeemer; the powers He designed for His service are used to oppose His grace and matchless love."—*Ibid.*, April 22, 1903.

"Satan urges before God his accusations against them, declaring that they have by their sins forfeited the divine protection, and claiming the right to destroy them as transgressors. He pronounces them just as deserving as himself of exclusion from the favor of God. *'Are these,'* he says, *'the people who are to take my place in heaven and the place of the angels who united with me?'* "—*Testimonies*, Vol. 5, p. 473.

"*Heaven will triumph; for the vacancies made in heaven by the fall of Satan and his angels will be filled by the redeemed of the Lord.*"—*S.D.A. Bible Commentary*, Vol. 7, p. 949.

"They [the Father and the Son] had wrought together in the creation of the earth and every living thing upon it."—*The Story of Redemption*, p. 20.

"Next to the angelic beings, the human family, formed in 'the image of God,' are the noblest of His created works."—*The Faith I Live By*, p. 29.

"In the divine plan, evil was foreseen and provided for. A remedy was provided sufficient for complete restoration. But in this plan, man himself must act a part."—*Signs of the Times*, April 22, 1903.

"We should consider that it was not merely to accomplish the redemption of man that Christ came to earth; it was not merely that the inhabitants of this little world might regard the law of God as it should be regarded; *but it was to demonstrate to all the worlds that God's law is unchangeable, and that the wages of sin is death.*

"There is a great deal more to this subject than we can take in at a glance. Oh that all might see the importance of carefully studying the Scriptures! Many seem to have the idea that this world and the heavenly mansions constitute the universe of God. Not so. The redeemed throng will range from world to world, and much of their time will be employed in searching out the mysteries of redemption. And throughout the whole stretch of eternity, this subject will be continually opening to their minds. The privileges of those who overcome by the blood of the Lamb and the word of their testimony are beyond comprehension."—*Review and Herald,* March 9, 1886.

## Supplementary Material for Chapter Four

"The Son of God is the center of the great plan of redemption which covers all dispensations. He is the 'Lamb slain from the foundation of the world.' He is the Redeemer of the fallen sons and daughters of Adam in all ages of human probation. 'Neither is there salvation in any other; for there is none other name under heaven given among men whereby we must be saved.' *Christ is the substance or body which casts its shadow back into former dispensations.*"—*Signs of the Times,* February 20, 1893.

"As time has rolled on from creation and the cross of Calvary, as prophecy has been and is still fulfilling, light and knowledge have greatly increased. But it does not become believers in God or the Bible to pour contempt on the age that has led step by step to the present. *In the life and death of Christ, a light flashes back upon the past, giving significance to the whole Jewish economy, and making of the old and the new dispensations a complete whole.* Nothing that God has ordained in the plan of redemption can be dispensed with. It is the working out of the divine will in the salvation of man."—*Review and Herald,* March 2, 1886.

"There is a day just about to burst upon us, when God's mysteries will be seen, and all His ways vindicated; when justice, mercy, and love will be the attributes of His throne. When the earthly warfare is accomplished, and the saints are all gathered home, our first theme will be the song of Moses, the servant of God. The second theme will be the song of the Lamb, the song of grace and redemption. This song will be louder, loftier, and in sublimer strains, echoing and reëchoing through the heavenly courts. *Thus the song of God's providence is sung, connecting the varying dispensations; for all is now seen without a veil between the legal, the prophetical, and the gospel.* The church history upon the earth, and the church redeemed in heaven, all center around the cross of Calvary. This is the theme, this is the song,—Christ all and in all,—in anthems of praise resounding through heaven from thousands and ten thousand times ten thousand and an innumerable company of the redeemed host. All unite in this song of Moses and of the Lamb. It is a new song, for it was never before sung in heaven."—*Testimonies to Ministers,* p. 433.

# Supplementary Material for Chapter Five

"The fragrant incense of the merits of Christ gives to the believing soul the virtues of His character. Thus it is that the co-operation of divine energy and merit with man makes him a complete overcomer in every sense, and *elevates* humanity in the scale of moral value with God."—*Review and Herald,* November 29, 1898.

"Christ's work was to reconcile *man to God* through His human nature, and *God to man* through His divine nature."—*Selected Messages,* Book One, p. 273.

"Thus Christ, in His own spotless righteousness, after shedding His precious blood, enters into the holy place to cleanse the sanctuary. And there the crimson current is brought into the service of *reconciling God to man.*"—*Testimonies,* Vol. 4, p. 122.

"Herein is the mystery of redemption, that the innocent, pure, and holy Son of the Infinite God was permitted to bear the punishment of a thankless race of rebels against the divine government; that through the manifestation of His matchless love, these rebels might stand before *Him* repentant, *forgiven, guiltless, as if they had never sinned.* Angels in heaven marveled that the wrath of God should be laid on His well beloved Son; that a life of infinite value in the heavenly courts should be given for the worthless life of a race degraded by sin."—*Bible Echo,* November 25, 1895.

"When Christ died upon the cross of Calvary, a new and living way was opened to both Jew and Gentile. The Saviour was henceforth to officiate as priest and advocate in the heaven of heavens. Henceforth the blood of beasts offered for sins was valueless, for the Lamb of God had died for the sins of the world."—Undated Manuscript 127. (*Questions on Doctrine,* p. 691.)

"It was the work of the priest in the daily ministration to present before God the blood of the sin-offering, also the incense which ascended with the prayers of Israel. *So did Christ plead His blood before the Father in behalf of sinners, and present before Him also, with the precious fragrance of His own righteousness, the prayers of penitent believers.* Such was the work of ministration in the first apartment of the sanctuary in heaven."—*The Great Controversy,* pp. 420, 421.

"For eighteen centuries this work of ministration continued in the first apartment of the sanctuary. The blood of Christ, pleaded in behalf of penitent believers, secured their pardon and acceptance with the Father, yet their sins still remained upon the books of record. As in the typical service there was a work of atonement at the close of the year, so before Christ's work for the redemption of men is completed, there is a work of atonement for the removal of sin from the sanctuary. This is the service which began when the 2300 days ended. At that time, as foretold by Daniel the prophet, our High Priest entered the most holy, to perform the last division of His solemn work,—to cleanse the sanctuary."—*Ibid.,* p. 421.

"As our Mediator, Jesus was fully able to accomplish this work of redemption; but O, at what a price! The sinless Son of God was condemned for the sin in which He had no part, in order that the sinner, through repentance and faith, might be justified by the righteousness of Christ, in which he had no personal merit. The sins of every one who has lived upon the earth were laid upon Christ, testifying to the fact that no one need be a loser in the conflict with Satan. Provision has been made that all may lay hold of the strength of Him who will save to the uttermost all who come unto God by Him.

"Christ receives upon Him the guilt of man's transgression, while He lays upon all who receive Him by faith, who return to their allegiance to God, His own spotless righteousness." —*Review and Herald*, May 23, 1899.(*Questions on Doctrine*, p. 689.)

## Supplementary Material for Chapter Six

"Let those who are oppressed under a sense of sin remember that there is hope for them. The salvation of the human race has ever been the object of the councils of heaven. The covenant of mercy was made before the foundation of the world. It has existed from all eternity, and is called the *everlasting covenant*. So surely as there never was a time when God was not, so surely there never was a moment when it was not the delight of the eternal mind to manifest His grace to humanity."—*S.D.A. Bible Commentary*, Vol. 7, p. 934. (*Signs of the Times*, June 12, 1901.)

"When they came to Sinai, he took occasion to refresh their minds in regard to his requirements. Christ and the Father, standing side by side upon the mount, with solemn majesty proclaimed the ten commandments, placing in the very center of the decalogue the Sabbath command."—*Historical Sketches*, p. 231.

"Israel was now to be taken into a close and peculiar relation to the Most High—to be incorporated as a church and a nation under the government of God. . . . Thus they entered into a solemn covenant with God, pledging themselves to accept Him as their ruler, by which they became, in a special sense, the subjects of His authority."—*Patriarchs and Prophets,* p. 303.

"The law and gospel are in perfect harmony. Each upholds the other. In all its majesty the law confronts the conscience, causing the sinner to feel his need of Christ as the propitiation for sin. The gospel recognizes the power and immutability of the law. 'I had not known sin, but by the law,' Paul declares (Romans 7:7). The sense of sin, urged home by the law, drives the sinner to the Saviour."—*Selected Messages,* Book One, p. 240.

## Supplementary Material for Chapter Seven

"The instant man accepted the temptations of Satan, and did the very things God had said he should not do, Christ, the Son of God, stood between the living and the dead, saying, 'Let the punishment fall on Me. I will stand in man's place. He shall have another chance.' "—*S.D.A. Bible Commentary,* Vol. 1, p. 1085.

"After the fall, Christ became Adam's instructor. He acted in God's stead toward humanity, saving the race from immediate death. He took upon Him the work of mediator between God and man."—*Ibid.,* Vol. 7, p. 912. (*Signs of the Times,* May 29, 1901.)

210

"Holy men of old were saved by faith in the blood of Christ. As they saw the dying agonies of the sacrificial victims, they looked across the gulf of ages to the Lamb of God that was to take away the sin of the world."—*The Acts of the Apostles,* pp. 424, 425.

"Adam listened to the words of the tempter, and yielding to his insinuations, fell into sin. Why was not the death penalty at once enforced in his case?—Because a ransom was found. God's only begotten Son volunteered to take the sin of man upon Himself, and to make an atonement for the fallen race. There could have been no pardon for sin had this atonement not been made. Had God pardoned Adam's sin without an atonement, sin would have been immortalized, and would have been perpetuated with a boldness that would have been without restraint."—*S.D.A. Bible Commentary,* Vol. 1, p. 1082. (*Review and Herald,* April 23, 1901.)

"Thus, through patriarchs and prophets, as well as through types and symbols, God spoke to the world concerning the coming of a Deliverer from sin."—*Prophets and Kings,* p. 697.

"Christ, in counsel with His Father, instituted the system of sacrificial offerings; that death, instead of being immediately visited upon the transgressor, should be transferred to a victim which should prefigure the great and perfect offering of the Son of God."—*Signs of the Times,* March 14, 1878. (*Questions on Doctrine,* p. 678.)

"The sins of the people were transferred in figure to the officiating priest, who was a mediator for the people. The priest could not himself become an offering for sin, and make an atonement with his life, for he was also a sinner. Therefore, instead of suffering death himself, he *{the priest}* killed a lamb without blemish; the penalty of sin was transferred to the innocent beast, which thus became his *{the priest's}* immediate substitute, and typified the perfect offering of Jesus Christ. Through the blood of this victim, man looked forward by faith to the blood of Christ which would atone for the sins of the world."—*Ibid.* (*Questions on Doctrine,* p. 669.)

"The Lord had made known to Adam, Abel, Seth, Enoch, Noah, Abraham, and the ancient worthies, especially Moses, that the ceremonial system of sacrifices and priesthood, of themselves, were not sufficient to secure the salvation of one soul. The system of sacrificial offerings pointed to Christ. Through these the ancient worthies saw Christ, and believed in Him. These were ordained of God to keep before the people the fearful separation which sin had made between God and man, requiring a mediating ministry. Through Christ, the communication which was cut off because of Adam's transgression, was opened between God and the ruined sinner. The infinite sacrifice that Christ voluntarily made for man remains a mystery that angels cannot fully fathom."—*Redemption: or the First Advent of Christ* (*Life of Christ,* Vol. 1), pp. 10, 11.

"In the earliest times every man was the priest of his own household. In the days of Abraham the priesthood was regarded as the birthright of the eldest son."—*Patriarchs and Prophets,* p. 350.

"Adam gladly received the welcome assurance of deliverance, and diligently instructed his children in the way of the

Lord. This promise was presented in close connection with the altar of sacrificial offerings. The altar and the promise stand side by side, and one casts clear beams of light upon the other, showing that the justice of an offended God could be appeased only by the death of His beloved Son. The bleeding victim consuming on the altar, illustrated Adam's teachings, and thus the sight of the eyes deepened the impression made by the hearing of the ear.

"Abel heard these precious lessons, and to him they were like seed sown on good ground."—*Signs of the Times,* December 23, 1886.

"In patriarchal times the sacrificial offerings connected with divine worship constituted a perpetual reminder of the coming of a Saviour, and thus it was with the entire ritual of the sanctuary services throughout Israel's history. In the ministration of the tabernacle, and of the temple that afterward took its place, the people were taught each day, by means of types and shadows, the great truths relative to the advent of Christ as Redeemer, Priest, and King; and once each year their minds were carried forward to the closing events of the great controversy between Christ and Satan, the final purification of the universe from sin and sinners."—*Prophets and Kings,* p. 684.

"He could lay down His life as priest and also victim. He possessed in Himself power to lay it down and take it up again. He offered Himself without spot to God."—Manuscript 92, 1899. (*Questions on Doctrine,* p. 666.)

"By faith Abel offered unto God a more excellent sacrifice than Cain. Hebrews 11:4. . . . Through the shed blood he looked to the future sacrifice, Christ dying on the cross of

Calvary; and trusting in the atonement that was there to be made, he had the witness that he was righteous, and his offering accepted."—*Patriarchs and Prophets,* p. 72.

"Cain and Abel were representatives of the two great classes. Abel, as priest, in solemn faith offered his sacrifice. Cain was willing to offer the fruit of his ground, but refused to connect with his offering the blood of beasts. . . . He refused to acknowledge his need of a Redeemer. This, to his proud heart, was dependence and humiliation."—*Redemption: or the Temptation of Christ (Life of Christ,* Vol. 1), p. 20.

"The infinite sufficiency of Christ is demonstrated by His bearing the sins of the whole world. He occupies the double position of offerer and of offering, of priest and of victim. He was holy, harmless, undefiled, and separate from sinners. 'The prince of this world cometh,' He declares, 'and findeth nothing in Me.' He was a Lamb without blemish, and without spot."—Letter 192, 1906. (*Questions on Doctrine,* p. 667.)

"As they saw the dying agonies of the sacrificial victims they looked across the gulf of ages to the Lamb of God that was to take away the sin of the world."—*The Acts of the Apostles,* pp. 424, 425.

"Man could not atone for man. His sinful, fallen condition would constitute him an imperfect offering, an atoning sacrifice of less value than Adam before his fall."—*The Spirit of Prophecy,* Vol. 2, p. 9. (*Questions on Doctrine,* p. 665.)

## Supplementary Material for Chapter Eight

"Another who came out to welcome the victorious patriarch was Melchizedek, king of Salem, who brought forth bread and wine for the refreshment of his army. As 'priest of the most high God,' he pronounced a blessing upon Abraham, and gave thanks to the Lord, who had wrought so great a deliverance by His servant. And Abraham 'gave him tithes of all.' "—*Patriarchs and Prophets,* p. 136.

"It was Christ that spoke through Melchizedek, the priest of the most high God. Melchizedek was not Christ, but he was the voice of God in the world, the representative of the Father. And all through the generations of the past, Christ has spoken; Christ has led His people, and has been the light of the world. When God chose Abraham as a representative of His truth, He took him out of his country, and away from his kindred, and set him apart."—*Selected Messages,* Book One, pp. 409, 410.

## Supplementary Material for Chapter Nine

"When our eyes look by faith into the sanctuary, and take in the reality, the importance and holiness, of the work there being done, everything of a selfish nature will be abhorred by us. Sin will appear as it is,—the transgression of God's holy law. The atonement will be better understood; and by living, active faith, we shall see that whatever of virtue humanity possesses, it exists only in Jesus Christ, the world's Redeemer." —*S.D.A. Bible Commentary,* Vol. 4, p. 1141.

*"We should not rest until we become intelligent in regard to the subject of the sanctuary, which is brought out in the visions of Daniel and John. . . .* God's people are now to have

their eyes fixed on the heavenly sanctuary, where the final ministration of our great High Priest in the work of the judgment is going forward,—where He is interceding for His people."—*Evangelism,* pp. 222, 223.

"The scenes connected with the sanctuary above should make such an impression upon the minds and hearts of all that they may be able to impress others. *All need to become more intelligent in regard to the work of the atonement, which is going on in the sanctuary above. When this grand truth is seen and understood, those who hold it will work in harmony with Christ to prepare a people to stand in the great day of God, and their efforts will be successful."—Testimonies,* Vol. 5, p. 575.

## Supplementary Material for Chapter Ten

"In the sacrificial offering on every altar was seen a Redeemer. With the cloud of incense arose from every contrite heart the prayer that God would accept their offerings as showing faith in the coming Saviour. Our Saviour has come and shed His blood as a sacrifice, and now He pleads that blood before His Father in the sanctuary in heaven. It is now, as anciently, only through the merits of that blood that the transgressor of God's law can find pardon. It is by exercising repentance toward God and faith in our Lord Jesus Christ." —*Review and Herald,* March 2, 1886.

"Holy men of old were saved by faith in the blood of Christ. As they saw the dying agonies of the sacrificial victims they looked across the gulf of ages to the Lamb of God that was to take away the sin of the world."—*The Acts of the Apostles,* pp. 424, 425.

# Supplementary Material for Chapter Eleven

"The church of God below is one with the church of God above. Believers on the earth and the beings in heaven who have never fallen constitute one church. Every heavenly intelligence is interested in the assemblies of the saints who on earth meet to worship God. In the inner court of heaven they listen to the testimony of the witnesses for Christ in the outer court on earth, and the praise and thanksgiving from the worshipers below is taken up in the heavenly anthem, and praise and rejoicing sound through the heavenly courts because Christ has not died in vain for the fallen sons of Adam. While angels drink from the fountainhead, the saints on earth drink of the pure streams flowing from the throne, the streams that make glad the city of our God. Oh, that we could all realize the nearness of heaven to earth!"

"The temple of God is opened in heaven, and the threshold is flushed with the glory which is for every church that will love God and keep His commandments. We need to study, to meditate, and to pray. Then we shall have spiritual eyesight to discern the inner courts of the celestial temple."—*Testimonies*, Vol. 6, pp. 366, 368.

"Our great High Priest has made the only sacrifice that is of any value in our salvation. When He offered Himself on the cross, a perfect atonement was made for the sins of the people. We are now standing in the outer court, waiting and looking for that blessed hope, the glorious appearing of our Lord and Saviour Jesus Christ. No sacrifices are to be offered without, for the great High Priest is performing His work in the most holy place."—*Signs of the Times*, June 28, 1899.

"Our great High Priest completed the sacrificial offering of Himself when He suffered without the gate. Then a perfect atonement was made for the sins of the people. Jesus is our Advocate, our High Priest, our Intercessor. Our present position therefore is like that of the Israelites, standing in the outer court, waiting and looking for that blessed hope, the glorious appearing of our Lord and Saviour Jesus Christ."—Manuscript 128, 1897. (*Questions on Doctrine,* pp. 663, 664.)

## Supplementary Material for Chapters Twelve and Thirteen

"The reconciliation of God to man, and man to God, is sure when certain conditions are met. The Lord says, 'The sacrifices of God are a broken spirit: a broken and a contrite heart, O God, Thou wilt not despise.' "—*Fundamentals of Christian Education,* pp. 370, 371.

"The humanity of Christ reached to the very depths of human wretchedness, and identified itself with the weaknesses and necessities of fallen man, while His divine nature grasped the Eternal. His work in bearing the guilt of man's transgression was not to give him license to continue to violate the law of God, which made man a debtor to the law, which debt Christ was Himself paying by His own suffering. The trials and sufferings of Christ were to impress man with a sense of his great sin in breaking the law of God, and to bring him to repentance and obedience to that law, and through obedience to acceptance with God. His righteousness He would impute to man, and thus raise him in moral value with God, so that his efforts to keep the divine law would be acceptable. *Christ's work was to reconcile man to God through His human*

218

*nature, and God to man through His divine nature."—Selected Messages,* Book One, pp. 272, 273.

"Christ has pledged Himself to be our Substitute and Surety, and He neglects no one. *There is an inexhaustible fund of perfect obedience accruing from His obedience.* In heaven His merits, His self-denial and self-sacrifice, are treasured up as incense to be offered up with the prayers of His people. As the sinner's sincere, humble prayers ascend to the throne of God, Christ mingles with them the merits of His life of perfect obedience."—*Review and Herald,* October 30, 1900.

"As the high priest sprinkled the warm blood upon the mercy-seat while the fragrant cloud of incense ascended before God, so, while we confess our sins and plead the efficacy of Christ's atoning blood, our prayers are to ascend to heaven, fragrant with the merits of our Saviour's character."—*Ibid.,* September 29, 1896. (*Questions on Doctrine,* pp. 668, 669.)

"While He took upon Him humanity, it was a life taken into union with Deity. *He could lay down His life as priest and also victim.* He possessed in Himself power to lay it down and take it up again. He offered Himself without spot to God." —Manuscript 92, 1899. (*Questions on Doctrine,* p. 666.)

"He [Jesus] fulfilled one phase of *His priesthood* by dying on the cross."—Manuscript 42, 1901. (*Questions on Doctrine,* p. 686.)

"*As the high priest laid aside his gorgeous pontifical robes, and officiated in the white linen dress of the common priest, so Christ took the form of a servant,* and offered sacrifice, Himself the priest, Himself the victim."—*The Desire of Ages,* p. 25.

"Still bearing humanity, He ascended to heaven, triumphant and victorious. He has taken the blood of His atonement into the holiest of all, *sprinkled it upon the mercy-seat and His own garments,* and blessed the people."—*The Youth's Instructor,* July 25, 1901.

"The law given upon Sinai was the enunciation of the principle of love—a revelation to earth of the law of heaven. It was ordained in the hand of a Mediator—spoken by Him through whose power the hearts of men could be brought into harmony with its principles. God had revealed the purpose of the law when He declared to Israel, 'Ye shall be holy men unto Me.' "—*Thoughts From the Mount of Blessing,* p. 46.

"Those only who acknowledge the binding claim of the moral law can explain the nature of the atonement. Christ came to mediate between God and man, *to make man one with God by bringing him into allegiance to His law.* There was no power in the law to pardon its transgressor. Jesus alone could pay the sinner's debt. But the fact that Jesus has paid the indebtedness of the repentant sinner does not give him license to continue in transgression of the law of God; but he must henceforth live in obedience to that law."—*Selected Messages,* Book One, pp. 229, 230. (*Signs of the Times,* March 14, 1878.)

"As the high priest, after performing his service in the holy of holies, came forth to the waiting congregation *in his pontifical robes,* so Christ will come the second time, clothed in garments of whitest white, 'so as no fuller on earth can white them.' (Mark 9:3.) He will come in His own glory, and in the glory of His Father, and all the angelic host will escort Him on His way."—*The Acts of the Apostles,* p. 33.

"Children of the Lord, how precious is the promise! How full the atonement of the Saviour for our guilt. The Redeemer, with a heart of unalterable love, *still sheds His sacred blood* in the sinner's behalf. The wounded hands, the pierced side, the marred feet, plead eloquently for fallen man, whose redemption is purchased at so great a cost. Oh, matchless condescension! Time nor events can lessen the efficacy of the atoning sacrifice. As the fragrant cloud of incense rose acceptably to heaven, and Aaron sprinkled the blood upon the mercy-seat of ancient Israel, and cleansed the people from guilt, so the merits of the slain Lamb are accepted by God to-day as a purifier from the defilement of sin."—*Review and Herald,* January 9, 1883.

"Type met antitype in the death of Christ, the Lamb slain for the sins of the world. Our great High Priest has made the only sacrifice that is of any value in our salvation. When He offered Himself on the cross, a perfect atonement was made for the sins of the people. *We are now standing in the outer court, waiting and looking for that blessed hope, the glorious appearing of our Lord and Saviour Jesus Christ.* No sacrifices are to be offered without, for the great High Priest is performing His work in the most holy place. In His intercession as our advocate, Christ needs no man's virtue, no man's intercession. He is the only sin-bearer, the only sin-offering. Prayer and confession are to be offered only to Him who has entered once

221

for all into the most holy place. He will save to the uttermost all who come to Him in faith. He ever liveth to make intercession for us."—*Signs of the Times*, June 28, 1899.

"The religious services, the prayers, the praise, the penitent confession of sin ascend from true believers as incense to the heavenly sanctuary, but passing through the corrupt channels of humanity, they are so defiled that unless purified by blood, they can never be of value with God. They ascend not in spotless purity, and unless the Intercessor, who is at God's right hand, presents and purifies all by His righteousness, it is not acceptable to God. All incense from earthly tabernacles must be moist with the cleansing drops of the blood of Christ. He holds before the Father the censer of His own merits, in which there is no taint of earthly corruption. He gathers into this censer the prayers, the praise, and the confessions of His people, and with these He puts His own spotless righteousness. Then, perfumed with the merits of Christ's propitiation, the incense comes up before God wholly and entirely acceptable. Then gracious answers are returned.

"Oh, that all may see that everything in obedience, in penitence, in praise and thanksgiving, must be placed upon the glowing fire of the righteousness of Christ. The fragrance of this righteousness ascends like a cloud around the mercy seat." —*Selected Messages*, Book One, p. 344.

"When you turn away from the broken cisterns that can hold no water, and in the name of Jesus your Advocate come directly to God, asking for the things you need, the righteousness of Christ will be revealed as your righteousness, the virtue of Christ as your virtue. You will then understand that justification will come alone through faith in Christ; for in Jesus is revealed the perfection of the character of God; in His life is manifested the outworking of the principles of holiness. Through the atoning blood of Christ the sinner is set free from bondage and condemnation; through the perfection of the sinless Substitute and Surety, he may run in the race of humble obedience to all of God's commandments. Without Christ he is under the condemnation of the law, always a sinner, but through faith in Christ he is made just before God."—*Ibid.,* p. 330.

"With the confession of the repenting, believing sinner, Christ mingles His own righteousness, that the prayer of fallen man may go up as fragrant incense before the Father, and the grace of God be imparted to the believing soul. Jesus says to the trembling, repenting soul: 'Let him take hold of my strength, that he may make peace with me; and he shall make peace with me' (Isaiah 27:5)."—*Ibid.,* p. 329.

"No man can look within himself and find anything in his character that will recommend him to God, or make his acceptance sure. It is only through Jesus, whom the Father gave for the life of the world, that the sinner may find access to God. Jesus alone is our Redeemer, our Advocate and Mediator; in Him is our only hope for pardon, peace, and righteousness. It is by virtue of the blood of Christ that the sin-stricken soul can be restored to soundness. Christ is the fragrance, the holy incense which makes your petition acceptable to the Father." —*Ibid.,* p. 332.

"The incense, ascending with the prayers of Israel, represents the merits and intercession of Christ, His perfect righteousness, which through faith is imputed to His people, and which can alone make the worship of sinful beings acceptable to God. Before the veil of the most holy place was an altar of perpetual intercession, before the holy, an altar of continual atonement. By blood and by incense God was to be approached —symbols pointing to the great Mediator, through whom sinners may approach Jehovah, and through whom alone mercy and salvation can be granted to the repentant, believing soul."—*Patriarchs and Prophets*, p. 353.

"As the priests morning and evening entered the holy place at the time of incense, the daily sacrifice was ready to be offered upon the altar in the court without. . . . Thus their petitions ascended with the cloud of incense, while faith laid hold upon the merits of the promised Saviour prefigured by the atoning sacrifice."—*Ibid.*

## Supplementary Material for Chapter Fourteen

"The crucifixion of Christ took place at the celebration of the Passover. At this time people from all parts of the world were assembled at Jerusalem. Representatives from foreign courts, kings, noblemen, princes, men who exerted a wide influence, witnessed the scenes of Christ's death. 'Lo, the kings were assembled, they passed by together. They saw it, and so they marveled; they were troubled, and hasted away.' It was then that Jehovah struck a blow that was felt to the remotest parts of the earth. The tidings of Christ's death were carried by strangers to every part of the world. This was the vital, all-absorbing truth on which God would have men in all ages fix their attention. He would have the death of His Son the great center of attraction."—*Signs of the Times*, January 4, 1899.

"While the people were assembling at Jerusalem to celebrate the Passover, He, the antitypical Lamb, by a voluntary act set Himself apart as an oblation."—*The Desire of Ages,* p. 571.

"While the westering sun was tinting and gilding the heavens, its resplendent glory lighted up the pure white marble of the temple walls, and sparkled on its gold-capped pillars." —*Ibid.,* p. 575.

"When the fast westering sun should pass from sight in the heavens, Jerusalem's day of grace would be ended."—*Ibid.,* p. 578.

"While the last rays of the setting sun were lingering on temple, tower, and pinnacle, would not some good angel lead her to the Saviour's love, and avert her doom? Beautiful and unholy city, that had stoned the prophets, that had rejected the Son of God, that was locking herself by her impenitence in fetters of bondage—her day of mercy was almost spent!" —*Ibid.*

"The observance of the Passover possessed a mournful interest to the Son of God. He saw in the slain lamb a symbol of His own death. The people who celebrated this ordinance were instructed to associate the slaying of the lamb with the future death of the Son of God."—*The Spirit of Prophecy,* Vol. 2, p. 36.

"The slaying of the Passover lamb was a shadow of the death of Christ. Says Paul, 'Christ our passover is sacrificed for us.' . . . On the fourteenth day of the first Jewish month, *the very day* and month on which, for fifteen long centuries, the Passover lamb had been slain, Christ, having eaten the Passover with His disciples instituted that feast which was to commemorate His own death as 'the Lamb of God, which taketh away the sin of the world.' "—*The Great Controversy*, p. 399.

"When the loud cry, 'It is finished,' came from the lips of Christ, the priests were officiating in the temple. *It was the hour of the evening sacrifice.* The lamb representing Christ had been brought to be slain. Clothed in his significant and beautiful dress, the priest stood with lifted knife, as did Abraham when he was about to slay his son. With intense interest the people were looking on. But the earth trembles and quakes; for the Lord Himself draws near. With a rending noise the inner veil of the temple is torn from top to bottom by an unseen hand, throwing open to the gaze of the multitude a place once filled with the presence of God. . . . All is terror and confusion. The priest is about to slay the victim; but the knife drops from his nerveless hand, and the lamb escapes. Type met antitype in the death of God's Son."—*The Desire of Ages*, pp. 756, 757.

"The Passover was to be both commemorative and typical, not only pointing back to the deliverance from Egypt, but forward to the greater deliverance which Christ was to accomplish in freeing His people from the bondage of sin. The sacrificial lamb represents 'the Lamb of God' in whom is our only hope of salvation. Says the apostle, 'Christ our Passover is sacrificed for us.' 1 Corinthians 5:7. It was not enough that the paschal lamb be slain; its blood must be sprinkled upon the doorposts; so the merits of Christ's blood must be applied to the soul. We must believe, not only that He died for the world, but that He died for us individually. We must appropriate to ourselves the virtue of the atoning sacrifice."—*Patriarchs and Prophets,* p. 277.

"The Jewish nation had been preserved as a witness that Christ was to be born of the seed of Abraham and of David's line; yet they knew not that His coming was now at hand. In the temple the morning and evening sacrifice daily pointed to the Lamb of God; yet even here was no preparation to receive Him. The priests and teachers of the nation knew not that the greatest event of the ages was to take place."—*The Desire of Ages,* p. 44.

"On the fourteenth day of the month, at even, the Passover was celebrated, its solemn, impressive ceremonies commemorating the deliverance from bondage in Egypt, and pointing forward to the sacrifice that should deliver from the bondage of sin. When the Saviour yielded up His life on Calvary, the significance of the Passover ceased, and the ordinance of the Lord's Supper was instituted as a memorial of the same event of which the Passover had been a type."—*Patriarchs and Prophets,* p. 539.

## Supplementary Material for Chapter Sixteen

"Christ was not alone in making His great sacrifice. It was the fulfillment of the covenant made between Him and His Father before the foundation of the world was laid. With clasped hands they had entered into the solemn pledge that Christ would become the surety for the human race if they were overcome by Satan's sophistry."—*The Faith I Live By,* p. 76. (*The Youth's Instructor,* June 14, 1900.)

"The Roman power was the instrument in God's hand to prevent the Light of the world from going out in darkness. The cross was lifted, *according to the plan of God,* in the sight of all nations, tongues, and people, calling their attention to the Lamb of God that taketh away the sins of the world."— *The Spirit of Prophecy,* Vol. 3, p. 181.

"Humanity died; *divinity did not die.* In His divinity, Christ possessed the power to break the bonds of death. He declares that He has life in Himself to quicken whom He will. . . .

"Only He who alone hath immortality, dwelling in light and life, should say, 'I have power to lay it [my life] down, and I have power to take it again' (John 10:18)."—*Selected Messages,* Book One, p. 301. (*The Youth's Instructor,* August 4, 1898.)

"Even doubts assailed the dying Son of God. He could not see through the portals of the tomb. Bright hope did not present to Him His coming forth from the tomb a conqueror, and His Father's acceptance of His sacrifice. The sin of the world with all its terribleness was felt to the utmost by the Son of God. The displeasure of the Father for sin, and its penalty, which was death, were all that He could realize through this amazing darkness. He was tempted to fear that sin was so offensive in the sight of His Father that He could not be reconciled to His Son. The fierce temptation that His own Father had forever left Him, caused that piercing cry from the cross, 'My God, My God, why hast Thou forsaken Me?'

"Christ felt much as sinners will feel when the vials of God's wrath shall be poured out upon them. Black despair, like the pall of death, will gather about their guilty souls, and then they will realize to the fullest extent the sinfulness of sin. Salvation has been purchased for them by the suffering and death of the Son of God. It might be theirs if they would accept of it willingly, gladly; but none are compelled to yield obedience to the law of God. . . .

"Faith and hope trembled in the expiring agonies of Christ, because God had removed the assurance He had heretofore given His beloved Son of His approbation and acceptance. The Redeemer of the world then relied upon the evidences which had hitherto strengthened Him, that His Father accepted His labors and was pleased with His work. In His dying agony, as He yields up His precious life, *He has by faith alone to trust in Him whom it has ever been His joy to obey*. He is not cheered with clear, bright rays of hope on the right hand nor on the left. All is enshrouded in oppressive gloom. Amid the awful darkness which is felt even by sympathizing nature, the Redeemer drains the mysterious cup even to its dregs. Denied even bright hope and confidence in the triumph which will be His in the near future, He cries with a loud voice, 'Father, into Thy hands I commend My spirit.' He is acquainted with the character of His Father, His justice, His mercy and great love. In submission He drops into the hands of His Father. Amid the convulsions of nature are heard by the amazed spectators the dying words of the Man of Calvary, 'It is finished.' "—*Signs of the Times,* February 4, 1913.

"When the soldier pierced the side of Jesus as He hung upon the cross, there came out two distinct streams, one of blood, the other of water. *The blood was to wash away the sins* of those who should believe in His name, and the water was to represent that living *water which is obtained from Jesus* to give life to the believer."—*Early Writings,* p. 209.

"God bowed His head satisfied. Now justice and mercy could blend. Now He could be just, and yet the Justifier of all who should believe on Christ. He [God] looked upon the victim expiring on the cross, and said, 'It is finished. The human race shall have another trial.' The redemption price was paid, and Satan fell like lightning from heaven."—*The Youth's Instructor,* June 21, 1900. (*Questions on Doctrine,* p. 674.)

"In the wilderness of temptation, in the Garden of Gethsemane, and on the cross, our Saviour measured weapons with the prince of darkness. His wounds became the trophies of His victory in behalf of the race. *When Christ hung in agony upon the cross, while evil spirits rejoiced and evil men reviled, then indeed His heel was bruised by Satan. But that very act was crushing the serpent's head.* Through death He destroyed 'him that had the power of death, that is, the devil.' Hebrews 2:14. This act decided the destiny of the rebel chief, and made forever sure the plan of salvation. In death He gained the victory over its power; in rising again, He opened the gates of the grave to all His followers. *In that last great contest we see fulfilled the prophecy, 'It shall bruise thy head, and thou shalt bruise his heel.' "*—*Prophets and Kings,* pp. 701, 702.

"By the offering made in our behalf we are placed on vantage-ground. The sinner, drawn by the power of Christ from the confederacy of sin, approaches the uplifted cross, and prostrates himself before it. Then there is a new creature in Christ Jesus. The sinner is cleansed and purified. A new heart is given him. Holiness finds that it has nothing more to re-

quire."—*General Conference Bulletin,* Fourth Quarter, 1899,
p. 102.

"To remove the cross from the Christian would be like
blotting the sun from the sky. The cross brings us near to God,
reconciling us to Him. . . . Without the cross, man could have
no union with the Father. *On it depends our every hope.*"
—*The Acts of the Apostles,* p. 209.

## Supplementary Material for Chapter Seventeen

"Christ had two natures, the nature of a man and the nature of God. In Him divinity and humanity were combined.
Upon His mediatorial work hangs the hope of the perishing
world. No one but Christ has ever succeeded in living a perfect life, in living a pure, spotless character. He exhibited a
perfect humanity, combined with deity; and by preserving
each nature distinct, He has given to the world a representation of the character of God and the character of a perfect
man. He shows us what God is, and what man may become—
godlike in character."—*General Conference Bulletin,* Fourth
Quarter, 1899, p. 102.

"After tempting man to sin, Satan claimed the earth as his,
and styled himself the prince of this world. *Having conformed
to his own nature the father and mother of our race, he
thought to establish here his empire.* He declared that men
had chosen him as their sovereign. Through his control of
men, he held dominion over the world."—*The Desire of Ages,*
pp. 114, 115.

"Christ came to the earth, taking humanity and standing

as man's representative, to show in the controversy with Satan that man, as God created him, connected with the Father and the Son, could obey every divine requirement."—*S.D.A. Bible Commentary,* Vol. 7, p. 926.

"Because of sin his [Adam's] posterity was born with inherent propensities of disobedience. But Jesus Christ was the only begotten Son of God. He took upon Himself human nature, and was tempted in all points as human nature is tempted. He could have sinned; He could have fallen, but not for one moment was there in Him an evil propensity."—*Ibid.,* Vol. 5, p. 1128.

"Christ came not confessing his own sins; but guilt was imputed to him as the sinner's substitute. He came not to repent on his own account; but in behalf of the sinner. As man had transgressed the law of God, Christ was to fulfill every requirement of that law, and thus show perfect obedience. 'Lo, I come to do thy will, O God!' Christ honored the ordinance of baptism by submitting to this rite. In this act he identified himself with his people as their representative and head. *As their substitute, he takes upon him their sins,* numbering himself with the transgressors, taking the steps the sinner is required to take, and doing the work the sinner must do."—*The Spirit of Prophecy,* Vol. 2, p. 59.

"Of the vast throng at the Jordan, few except John discerned the heavenly vision. Yet the solemnity of the divine Presence rested upon the assembly. The people stood silently gazing upon Christ. His form was bathed in the light that ever surrounds the throne of God. His upturned face was glorified as they had never before seen the face of man. From the open heavens a voice was heard saying, 'This is My beloved Son, in whom I am well pleased.'

"These words of confirmation were given to inspire faith in those who witnessed the scene, and to strengthen the Saviour for His mission. *Notwithstanding that the sins of a guilty world were laid upon Christ, notwithstanding the humiliation of taking upon Himself our fallen nature,* the voice from heaven declared Him to be the Son of the Eternal."—*The Desire of Ages,* p. 112.

"When His ministry commenced, after His baptism, He endured an agonizing fast of nearly six weeks. It was not merely the gnawing pangs of hunger which made His sufferings inexpressibly severe, but it was the guilt of the sins of the world which pressed so heavily upon Him. *He who knew no sin was made sin for us. With this terrible weight of guilt upon Him because of our sins* He withstood the fearful test upon appetite, and upon love of the world and of honor, and pride of display which leads to presumption."—*Testimonies,* Vol. 3, p. 372.

## Supplementary Material for Chapter Eighteen

"As the sin bearer, and priest and representative of man before God, He [Christ] entered into the life of humanity, bearing our flesh and blood."—*S.D.A. Bible Commentary,* Vol. 7, p. 925. (Letter 97, 1898.)

"The child for whom the redemption money had been paid was He who was to pay the ransom for the sins of the whole world. He was the true 'high priest over the house of God,' the head of 'an unchangeable priesthood,' the intercessor at 'the right hand of the Majesty on high.' "—*The Desire of Ages,* pp. 52, 55.

"Christ was not alone in making His great sacrifice. It was the fulfillment of the covenant made between Him and His Father before the foundation of the world was laid. With clasped hands they had entered into the solemn pledge that Christ would become the surety for the human race if they were overcome by Satan's sophistry."—*The Faith I Live By,* p. 76. (*The Youth's Instructor,* June 14, 1900.)

"Justice demanded the sufferings of a man. Christ, equal with God, gave the sufferings of a God. He needed no atonement. His suffering was not for any sin He had committed; it was for man—all for man; and His free pardon is accessible to all. The suffering of Christ was in correspondence with His spotless purity; His depth of agony, proportionate to the dignity and grandeur of His character."—*Review and Herald,* September 21, 1886. (*Questions on Doctrine,* p. 677.)

"The divine Son of God was the only sacrifice of sufficient value to fully satisfy the claims of God's perfect law. The angels were sinless, but of less value than the law of God. They were amenable to law. They were messengers to do the will of Christ, and before Him to bow. They were created beings, and probationers. Upon Christ no requirements were laid. He had power to lay down His life, and to take it again. No obligation was laid upon Him to undertake the work of atonement. It was a voluntary sacrifice that He made. His life was of sufficient value to rescue man from his fallen condition."—*Review and Herald,* December 17, 1872. (*Questions on Doctrine,* p. 677.)

"He fulfilled one phase of His priesthood by dying on the

cross for the fallen race."—Manuscript 42, 1901. (*Questions on Doctrine,* p. 686.)

"In His humiliation He as a prophet had addressed the daughters of Jerusalem; as priest and advocate He had pleaded with the Father to forgive His murderers; as a loving Saviour He had forgiven the sins of the penitent thief."—*The Desire of Ages,* p. 752.

"The infinite sufficiency of Christ is demonstrated by His bearing the sins of the whole world. He occupies the double position of offerer and of offering, of priest and of victim. He was holy, harmless, undefiled, and separate from sinners." —Letter 192, 1906. (*Questions on Doctrine,* p. 667.)

"As the high priest laid aside his gorgeous pontifical robes, and officiated in the white linen dress of a common priest, so Christ emptied Himself, and took the form of a servant, and offered the sacrifice, Himself the priest, Himself the victim."—*The Southern Watchman,* August 6, 1903. (*Questions on Doctrine,* p. 667.)

"By His perfect obedience He has satisfied the claims of the law, and my only hope is found in looking to Him as my substitute and surety, who obeyed the law perfectly for me. By faith in His merits I am free from the condemnation of the law. He clothes me with His righteousness, which answers all the demands of the law. I am complete in Him who brings in everlasting righteousness. He presents me to God in the spotless garment of which no thread was woven by any human agent."—*Selected Messages,* Book One, p. 396.

## Supplementary Material for Chapter Nineteen

"Christ came not confessing His own sins; but guilt was imputed to Him as the sinner's substitute. *He came not to repent on His own account; but in behalf of the sinner.* As man had transgressed the law of God, Christ was to fulfill every requirement of that law, and thus show perfect obedience. 'Lo, I come to do thy will, O God!' Christ honored the ordinance of baptism by submitting to this rite. In this act He identified Himself with His people as their representative and head. As their substitute He takes upon Him their sins, numbering Himself with the transgressors, taking the steps the sinner is required to take, and doing the work the sinner must do."—*The Spirit of Prophecy,* Vol. 2, p. 59.

"Ever since Adam's sin, the human race had been cut off from direct communion with God; the intercourse between heaven and earth had been through Christ; but now that Jesus had come 'in the likeness of sinful flesh' (Romans 8:3), the Father Himself spoke. He had before communicated with humanity *through* Christ; but now He communicated *in* Christ. . . . Now it was manifest that the connection between God and man had been restored."—*The Desire of Ages,* p. 116.

"What does this scene mean to us? How thoughtlessly we have read the account of the baptism of our Lord, not realizing that *its significance was of the greatest importance to us,* and that Christ was accepted of the Father in man's behalf. As Jesus bowed on the banks of Jordan and offered up His petition, humanity was presented to the Father by Him who had clothed His divinity with humanity. Jesus offered Himself to the Father in man's behalf, that those who had been separated from God through sin, might be brought back to God through the merits of the divine Petitioner. . . . The prayer of Christ in behalf of lost humanity cleaved its way through every shadow that Satan had cast between man and God, and left a clear channel of communication to the very throne of glory. The gates were left ajar, the heavens were opened."—*S.D.A. Bible Commentary*, Vol. 5, p. 1078. (*Signs of the Times,* April 18, 1892.)

"When He was baptized, the heavenly host knew that Jesus had placed His feet in the blood-stained path that led to Calvary."—*The Youth's Instructor,* June 23, 1892.

" 'This is my beloved Son, in whom I am well pleased.' How many have read over this relation, and have not had their hearts stirred by its significant truths! Many have thought that it did not concern mankind; but *it is of the greatest importance to each one of them.* Jesus was accepted of Heaven as a representative of the human race; with all our sin and weakness, we are not cast aside as worthless; we are accepted in the Beloved; for heaven has been opened to our petitions through the Son of God."—*Signs of the Times,* July 28, 1890.

"That prayer was for us; the answer was for us, it testifies that you are accepted in the Beloved. That very prayer that entered heaven, bears upward your prayers, my prayers, and the prayers of every soul that comes to God with a hungering and thirsting after righteousness. The merit of Jesus, His righteousness, gives fragrance to our prayers as holy incense that ascends to God."—*Bible Echo,* November 12, 1894, p. 7.

"A new and important era was opening before Him. . . . As one with us, He must bear the burden of our guilt and woe. *The Sinless One must feel* the shame of sin."—*The Desire of Ages,* p. 111.

"He who knew no sin, became sin for the race, that His righteousness might be imputed to man. Through the perfection of Christ's character, man was elevated in the scale of moral value with God; and through the merits of Christ, finite man was linked to the Infinite. Thus the gulf which sin had made was bridged by the world's Redeemer.

"But few have a true sense of the great privileges which Christ gained for man by thus opening heaven before him. The Son of God was then the representative of our race; and the special power and glory which the Majesty of Heaven conferred upon Him, and His words of approval, are the surest pledge of His love and good will to man. As Christ's intercessions in our behalf were heard, the evidence was given to man that God will accept our prayers in our own behalf through the name of Jesus. The continued, earnest prayer of faith will bring us light and strength to withstand the fiercest assaults of Satan."—*The Sufferings of Christ,* p. 8.

"Christ, the great anti-type, both Sacrifice and High Priest, clothed in His own spotless righteousness, was soon to be slain as a lamb without blemish, for the sins of the world." —*Signs of the Times,* September 19, 1892.

"The infinite sufficiency of Christ is demonstrated by His bearing the sins of the whole world. He *occupies the double position of offerer and of offering,* of priest and of victim. . . .

238

He was a Lamb without blemish, and without spot."—Letter 192, 1906. (*Questions on Doctrine,* p. 667.)

## Supplementary Material for Chapter Twenty

"The great work of redemption could be carried out only by the Redeemer taking the place of fallen Adam. *With the sins of the world laid upon Him,* He would go over the ground where Adam stumbled. He would bear a test infinitely more severe than that which Adam failed to endure. *He would overcome on man's account,* and conquer the tempter, that, through His obedience, His purity of character and steadfast integrity, His righteousness might be imputed to man, that, through His name, man might overcome the foe on his own account."—*Redemption: or the Temptation of Christ (Life of Christ,* Vol. 1), pp. 14, 15.

"It is impossible for man to know the strength of Satan's temptations to the Son of God. Every temptation that seems so afflicting to man in his daily life, so difficult to resist and overcome, was brought to bear upon the Son of God in as much greater degree as His excellence of character was superior to that of fallen man."—*Ibid.,* p. 29.

"As soon as the long fast of Christ commenced, Satan was at hand with his temptations. He came to Christ, enshrouded in light, claiming to be one of the angels from the throne of God, sent upon an errand of mercy to sympathize with Him, and to relieve Him of His suffering condition. He tried to make Christ believe that God did not require Him to pass through the self-denial and sufferings He anticipated; that he had been sent from heaven to bear to Him the message, that God only designed to prove His willingness to endure.

"Satan told Christ that He was to set His feet in the blood-stained path, but not to travel it, that, like Abraham, He was tested to show His perfect obedience. He also stated that he was the angel that stayed the hand of Abraham as the knife was raised to slay Isaac, and he had now come to save His life; that it was not necessary for Him to endure this painful hunger and death from starvation; and that he would help Him bear the work in the plan of salvation."

"Christ knew that Satan was a liar from the beginning, and it required strong self-control to listen to the propositions of this insulting deceiver, and not instantly rebuke his bold assumptions. Satan was expecting that the Son of God would, in His extreme weakness and agony of spirit, give him an opportunity to obtain advantage over Him. He designed to pervert the words of Christ and claim advantage, and call to his aid his fallen angels to use their utmost power to prevail against and overcome Him."—*Ibid.*, pp. 37, 43, 44.

"It was not the gnawing pangs of hunger alone which made the sufferings of our Redeemer so inexpressibly severe. *It was the sense of guilt* which had resulted from the indulgence of appetite that had brought such terrible woe into the world, which pressed so heavily upon His divine soul. 'For he hath made him to be sin for us, who knew no sin; that we might be made the righteousness of God in him.'

"With man's nature, *and the terrible weight of his sins pressing upon Him*, our Redeemer withstood the power of Satan upon this great leading temptation, which imperils the souls of men. If man should overcome this temptation, he could conquer on every other point.

"Intemperance lies at the foundation of all the moral evils known to man. Christ began the work of redemption just where the ruin began. The fall of our first parents was caused by the indulgence of appetite. *In redemption, the denial of appetite is the first work of Christ.* What amazing love has Christ manifested in coming into the world to bear our sins and infirmities, *and to tread the path of suffering,* that He might show us by His life of spotless merit how we should walk, and overcome as He had overcome, and that we might become reconciled to God."—*The Sufferings of Christ,* pp. 11, 12.

"Satan tempted the first Adam in Eden, and Adam reasoned with the enemy, thus giving him the advantage. *Satan exercised his power of hypnotism over Adam and Eve, and this power he strove to exercise over Christ.* But after the word of Scripture was quoted, Satan knew that he had no chance of triumphing."—*S.D.A. Bible Commentary,* Vol. 5, p. 1081.

"The great trial of Christ in the wilderness on the point of appetite was to leave man an example of self-denial. This long fast was to convict men of sinfulness of the things in which professed Christians indulge. The victory which Christ gained in the wilderness was to show man the sinfulness of the very things in which he takes such pleasure. *The salvation of man was in the balance, and to be decided by the trial of Christ in the wilderness.* If Christ was a victor on the point of appetite, then there was a chance for man to overcome. If Satan gained the victory through his subtlety, man was bound, by the power of appetite, in chains of indulgence which he could not have moral power to break. *Christ's humanity alone could never have endured this test, but His divine power, combined with humanity, gained in behalf of man an infinite victory.* Our representative in this victory raised humanity in the scale of moral value with God."—*Signs of the Times,* March 4, 1913.

"Professed Christians, who enjoy gatherings of gaiety, pleasure, and feasting, cannot appreciate the conflict of Christ in the wilderness. This example of their Lord in overcoming Satan is lost to them. This infinite victory which Christ achieved for them in the plan of salvation, is meaningless. They have no special interest in the wonderful humiliation of our Saviour, and the anguish and sufferings He endured for sinful man, while Satan was pressing Him with his manifold temptations. *The scene of trial with Christ in the wilderness* was the foundation of the plan of salvation, and gives to fallen man the key whereby he, in Christ's name, may overcome." —*Redemption: or the Temptation of Christ (Life of Christ,* Vol. 1), pp. 63, 64.

"But many of you say, 'How can I help sinning? I have tried to overcome, but I do not make advancement.' You never can in your own strength, you will fail; but help is laid upon One who is mighty. In His strength you may be more than conqueror. You should arise and say, 'Through the grace of God, I will be an overcomer.' Put your will on the side of God's will, and with your eye fixed upon Him who is the author and finisher of your faith, you may make straight paths for your feet. When you are tempted, say, 'Jesus is my Saviour, I love Him, because He has first loved me.' Show that you trust Him. As you walk the streets, as you work about your house, you can communicate with your Lord. Lay hold upon Him by living faith, and believe the word of God to the letter. . . . Say, 'I will be free, *I am free;*' and when Satan tells you that you are a sinner, tell him, 'I know it, but Jesus said, "I am not

come to call the righteous, but sinners to repentance." ' "
—*Review and Herald,* September 20, 1892. (Quoted in
*Review and Herald,* May 15, 1919, p. 14.)

"It was a difficult task for the Prince of Life to carry out
the plan which He had undertaken for the salvation of man,
in clothing His divinity with humanity. . . . It was as difficult
for Him to keep the level of humanity as for men to rise above
the low level of their depraved natures, and be partakers of
the divine nature. . . .

"Adam was not deceived by the serpent, as was Eve, and it
was inexcusable in Adam to rashly transgress God's positive
command. Adam was presumptuous because his wife had
sinned. He could not see what would become of Eve. He was
sad, troubled, and tempted. . . . Doubts arose in his mind in
regard to whether God did mean just as He said. He rashly
ate the tempting fruit."—*Redemption: or the Temptation of
Christ* (*Life of Christ,* Vol. 1), pp. 87, 88.

"Think of Christ's humiliation. He took upon Himself
fallen, suffering human nature, degraded and defiled by sin.
He took our sorrows, bearing our grief and shame. He endured
all the temptations wherewith man is beset. He united humanity with divinity: a divine spirit dwelt in a temple of flesh.
He united Himself with the temple. 'The Word was made
flesh, and dwelt among us,' because by so doing He could associate with the sinful, sorrowing sons and daughters of Adam."
—*S.D.A. Bible Commentary,* Vol. 4, p. 1147. (*The Youth's
Instructor,* December 20, 1900.)

"The admonition of the Saviour is, 'Watch and pray, that
ye enter not into temptation.' If Satan cannot prevent persons

from exercising faith, he will try to lead them to presume upon the willingness and power of God, by placing themselves unnecessarily in the way of temptation. *Presumption is a most common temptation, and as Satan assails men with this, he obtains the victory nine times out of ten.* Those who profess to be followers of Christ, and who claim by their faith to be enlisted in the warfare against all evil in their nature, frequently plunge without thought into temptations from which it would require a miracle to bring them forth unsullied. Meditation and prayer would have preserved them from these temptations by leading them to shun the critical, dangerous position in which they placed themselves."—"Practical Addresses," in *Historical Sketches,* p. 133.

"Christ was suffering as the members of the human family suffer under temptation; but it was not the will of God that He should exercise His divine power in His own behalf. Had He not stood as our representative, Christ's innocence would have exempted Him from all this anguish; but it was because of His innocence that He felt so keenly the assaults of Satan. All the suffering that is the result of sin was poured into the bosom of the sinless Son of God. Satan was bruising the heel of Christ; but every pang endured by Christ, every grief, every disquietude, was fulfilling the great plan of man's redemption. Every blow inflicted by the enemy was rebounding on himself. Christ was bruising the serpent's head."—*The Youth's Instructor,* December 21, 1899.

## Supplementary Material for Chapter Twenty-one

"We need to be enlightened in regard to the plan of salvation. There is not one in one hundred who understands for himself the Bible truth on this subject that is so necessary to our present and eternal welfare. When light begins to shine forth to make clear the plan of redemption to the people, the enemy works with all diligence that the light may be shut away from the hearts of men."—*Selected Messages,* Book One, p. 360.

"The understanding of the people of God has been blinded, for Satan has misrepresented the character of God. Our good and gracious Lord has been presented before the people clothed in the attributes of Satan, and men and women who have been seeking for truth, have so long regarded God in a false light that it is difficult to dispel the cloud that obscures His glory from their view. Many have been living in an atmosphere of doubt, and it seems almost impossible for them to lay hold on the hope set before them in the gospel of Christ." —*Ibid.,* p. 355.

"The salvation of the human race has ever been the object of the councils of heaven. . . . So surely as there never was a time when God was not, so surely there never was a moment when it was not the delight of the eternal mind to manifest His grace to humanity."—*S.D.A. Bible Commentary,* Vol. 7, p. 934.

"Many have confused ideas in regard to conversion. They have often heard the words repeated from the pulpit, 'Ye must be born again.' 'You must have a new heart.' These expressions have perplexed them. They could not comprehend the plan of salvation.

"Many have stumbled to ruin because of the erroneous

doctrines taught by some ministers concerning the change that takes place at conversion. . . . They are waiting for that peculiar change that they have been led to believe is connected with conversion. . . .

"Failing to understand the simplicity of the plan of salvation, they lost many privileges and blessings which they might have claimed had they only believed, when they first turned to God, that He had accepted them."—*Evangelism*, p. 286.

"Paul the apostle . . . longed for the purity, the righteousness, to which in himself he was powerless to attain, and cried out, 'O wretched man that I am! who shall deliver me from this body of death?' Romans 7:24, margin. Such is the cry that has gone up from burdened hearts in all lands and in all ages. To all, there is but one answer, 'Behold the Lamb of God, which taketh away the sin of the world.' John 1:29."—*Steps to Christ*, pp. 18, 19.

"*Through this simple act of believing God,* the Holy Spirit has begotten a new life in your heart. You are as a child born into the family of God, and He loves you as He loves His Son." —*Ibid.*, pp. 51, 52.

"Go to Him, and ask that He will wash away your sins and give you a new heart. Then believe that He does this *because He has promised.* . . . It is our privilege to go to Jesus and be cleansed, and to stand before the law without shame or remorse."—*Ibid.*, pp. 49-51.

"When at the foot of the cross the sinner looks up to the One who died to save him, he may rejoice with fullness of joy; for his sins are pardoned. *Kneeling in faith at the cross, he has reached the highest place to which man can attain."* —*The Acts of the Apostles,* pp. 209, 210.

"It is in looking upon our sinful condition, and talking and mourning over our wretchedness, that distress becomes more keen, and pain accumulates. Let the sinner arise in the strength of Jesus, for he has no strength of his own, and let him assert his liberty. Let him believe that the Lord has spoken truth, and trust in Him, whatever may be the feelings of the heart. . . .

"All legalism, all the sorrow and woe by which you may encompass yourself, will not give you one moment of relief. *You cannot rightly estimate sin.* You must accept God's estimate, and it is heavy indeed. If you bore the guilt of your sin, it would crush you; but the sinless One has taken your place, and, though undeserving, He has borne your guilt. By accepting the provision God has made, you may stand free before God in the merit and virtue of your Substitute. You will then have a proper estimate of sin, and the godly sorrow of true repentance will take the place of hopeless discouragement and grief, for you will turn from sin with grief and abhorrence. . . .

"God does not ask you to *feel* that Jesus is your Saviour, but to *believe* that He died for you, and that His blood now cleanseth you from all sin. You have been bitten by the serpent, and as the serpent was lifted up in the wilderness that the dying might look and live, so Christ was lifted up, that whosoever believeth in Him should not perish, but have eternal life. *Saving faith is simplicity itself.* . . . Look to the uplifted Saviour, and, however grievous may have been your sins, *believe He saves you."*—*Signs of the Times,* April 9, 1894.

"As the sinner, drawn by the love of Christ, approaches the cross, and prostrates himself before it, there is a new creation. A new heart is given him. He becomes a new creature in Christ Jesus. *Holiness finds that it has nothing more to require.* . . . Great as is the shame and degradation through sin, even greater will be the honor and exaltation through redeeming love. To human beings striving for conformity to the divine image, there is imparted an outlay of heavenly treasures, and excellency of power, that will place them higher than even the angels who have never sinned."—*Ibid.*, June 4, 1902.

"A much finer material will compose the human body, for it is a new creation, *a new birth.*"—*S.D.A. Bible Commentary,* Vol. 6, p. 1093.

## Supplementary Material for Chapter Twenty-two

"Christ did not come to change the Sabbath of the fourth commandment; He did not come to weaken or set aside the law of God in one particular; He came to express in His own person the love of God, and to vindicate every precept of the holy law. Instead of abrogating the law to meet man in his fallen condition, Christ maintained its sacred dignity.

"The Lord does not save sinners by abrogating His law, the foundation of His government in heaven and earth. God is a Judge, the guardian of justice. The transgression of His law in a single instance, in the smallest particular, is sin. God can not dispense with His law, He can not do away with its smallest item, in order to pardon sin. The justice, the moral excellence, of the law must be maintained and vindicated before the heavenly universe. And that holy law could not be main-

tained at any smaller price than the death of the Son of God."
—*Review and Herald,* November 15, 1898.

"Those who in the face of these specifications refuse to
repent of their transgressions will realize the result of disobedience. Individually we need to inquire, In observing a day of
rest, have I drawn my faith from the Scriptures, or from a
spurious representation of truth? Every soul who fastens himself to the divine, everlasting covenant, made and presented to
us as a sign and mark of God's government, fastens himself to
the golden chain of obedience, *every link of which is a promise.* He shows that he regards God's Word as above the word
of man, God's love as preferable to the love of man. And those
who repent of transgression, and return to their loyalty by
accepting God's mark, show themselves to be true subjects,
ready to do His will, to obey His commandments. True observance of the Sabbath is the sign of loyalty to God."—*S.D.A.
Bible Commentary,* Vol. 7, p. 981.

## Supplementary Material for
## Chapter Twenty-three

"If you give yourself to Him, and accept Him as your
Saviour, then, sinful as your life may have been, for His sake
you are accounted righteous. *Christ's character stands in place
of your character,* and you are accepted before God just as if
you had not sinned."—*Steps to Christ,* p. 62.

"The righteousness by which we are justified is imputed;
the righteousness by which we are sanctified is imparted. The
first is our title to heaven, the second is our fitness for heaven."
—*Messages to Young People,* p. 35.

249

"The proud heart strives to earn salvation; but both our title to heaven and our fitness for it are found in the righteousness of Christ."—*The Desire of Ages*, p. 300.

"Bear in mind, the time will never come when the hellish shadow of Satan will not be cast athwart our pathway to obstruct our faith, and eclipse the light emanating from the presence of Jesus, the Sun of Righteousness. *Our faith must not stagger, but cleave through that shadow*."—*Testimonies to Ministers*, p. 387.

"It is the grace that Christ implants in the soul which creates in man enmity against Satan. Without this converting grace and renewing power, man would continue the captive of Satan, a servant ever ready to do his bidding. But the new principle in the soul creates conflict where hitherto had been peace. The power which Christ imparts enables man to resist the tyrant and usurper. Whoever is seen to abhor sin instead of loving it, whoever resists and conquers those passions that have held sway within, displays the operation of a principle wholly from above."—*Signs of the Times*, February 17, 1909.

"Many are losing the right way, in consequence of thinking that they must climb to heaven, that they must do something to merit the favor of God."—*Selected Messages*, Book One, p. 368.

"We can do nothing, *absolutely nothing*, to commend ourselves to divine favor."—*Ibid.*, pp. 353, 354.

"Some who come to God by repentance and confession, and even believe that their sins are forgiven, still fail of claiming, as they should, the promises of God. They do not see that Jesus is an ever-present Saviour; and they are not ready to commit the keeping of their souls to Him, relying upon Him to perfect the work of grace begun in their hearts. *While they think they are committing themselves to God, there is a great deal of self-dependence.* There are conscientious souls that trust partly to God, and partly to themselves. They do not look to God, to be kept by His power, but depend upon watchfulness against temptation, and the performance of certain duties for acceptance with Him. *There are no victories in this kind of faith.*"—*Ibid.,* p. 353.

"The part man has to act in the salvation of the soul is to believe on Jesus Christ as a perfect Redeemer, not for some other man, but for his own self."—*The Faith I Live By,* p. 115.

"Instead of going about to establish our own righteousness we accept the righteousness of Christ. His blood atones for our sins. *His obedience is accepted for us.*"—*Patriarchs and Prophets,* p. 372.

"We must learn in the school of Christ. Nothing but His righteousness can entitle us to one of the blessings of the covenant of grace. We have long desired and tried to obtain these blessings, *but have not received them because we have cherished the idea that we could do something to make ourselves worthy of them.*"—*Selected Messages,* Book One, p. 351.

"There are those who have known the pardoning love of Christ and who really desire to be children of God, yet they realize that their character is imperfect, their life faulty, and they are ready to doubt whether their hearts have been renewed by the Holy Spirit. To such I would say, Do not draw back in despair. *We shall often have to bow down and weep at the feet of Jesus because of our shortcomings and mistakes, but we are not to be discouraged.* Even if we are overcome by the enemy, we are not cast off, not forsaken and rejected of God. No; Christ is at the right hand of God, who also maketh intercession for us."—*Steps to Christ,* p. 64.

"There are conditions to our receiving justification and sanctification, and the righteousness of Christ. . . . While good works will not save even one soul, yet it is impossible for even one soul to be saved without good works. God saves us under a law, that we must ask if we would receive, seek if we would find, and knock if we would have the door opened unto us." —*Selected Messages,* Book One, p. 377.

"*When it is in the heart to obey God,* when efforts are put forth to this end, Jesus accepts this disposition and effort as man's best service, and He makes up for the deficiency with His own divine merit."—*Ibid.,* p. 382.

"Paul's sanctification was a constant conflict with self. Said he: 'I die daily.' *His will and his desires every day conflicted with duty and the will of God.* Instead of following inclination, he did the will of God, however unpleasant and crucifying to his nature."—*Testimonies,* Vol. 4, p. 299.

"The tempter often works most successfully through those who are least suspected of being under his control. . . . Many a man of cultured intellect and pleasant manners, who would not stoop to what is commonly regarded as an immoral act, is but a polished instrument in the hands of Satan. The insidious, deceptive character of his influence and example renders him a more dangerous enemy to the cause of Christ than are those who are ignorant and uncultured."—*The Great Controversy,* p. 509.

"The strongest bulwark of vice in our world is not the iniquitous life of the abandoned sinner or the degraded outcast; it is that life which otherwise appears virtuous, honorable, and noble, but in which one sin is fostered, one vice indulged. To the soul that is struggling in secret against some giant temptation, trembling upon the very verge of the precipice, such an example is one of the most powerful enticements to sin. He who, endowed with high conceptions of life and truth and honor, does yet willfully transgress one precept of God's holy law, has perverted His noble gifts into a lure to sin. *Genius, talent, sympathy, even generous and kindly deeds, may become decoys of Satan to entice other souls* over the precipice of ruin for this life and the life to come."—*Thoughts From the Mount of Blessing,* pp. 94, 95.

"God always demanded good works, the law demands it, but because man placed himself in sin where his good works were valueless, Jesus' righteousness alone can avail. . . . All that man can possibly do toward his own salvation is to accept the invitation, 'Whosoever will, let him take the water of life freely.' Revelation 22:17. No sin can be committed by man for which satisfaction has not been met on Calvary. Thus the cross, in earnest appeals, continually proffers to the sinner a thorough expiation."—*Selected Messages,* Book One, p. 343.

"While God can be just, and yet justify the sinner through the merits of Christ, no man can cover his soul with the garments of Christ's righteousness while practicing known sins, or neglecting known duties."—*The Faith I Live By,* p. 115.

"There is nothing so offensive to God, or so dangerous to the human soul as pride and self-sufficiency. Of all sins it is the most hopeless, the most incurable."—*Christ's Object Lessons,* p. 154.

"To esteem others better than themselves is a great trial to those who are naturally self-inflated. . . . Faith that produces love to God and love to our neighbor is true faith. This faith will lead to genuine sanctification."—*Signs of the Times,* February 24, 1890.

"Unbelief is the sin that so easily besets us; and this sin is obnoxious to God. However secret is its working in the heart, the guilty one stands revealed and convicted before heaven. The Redeemer of the world has pledged His word, saying, 'Ask, and it shall be given you.' Is it any marvel then that the blessing of God is withheld when you dishonor His name by your unbelief?"—*Ibid.,* September 12, 1892.

"While we cannot claim perfection of the flesh, we may have Christian perfection of the soul. Through the sacrifice made in our behalf, sins may be perfectly forgiven. Our dependence is not in what man can do; it is in what God can do for man through Christ. When we surrender ourselves wholly to God, and fully believe, the blood of Christ cleanses from all sin. The conscience can be freed from condemnation. Through faith in His blood, all may be made perfect in Christ Jesus. Thank God that we are not dealing with impossibilities. *We may claim sanctification.* We may enjoy the favor of God. We are not to be anxious about what Christ and God think of us, but about what God thinks of Christ, our Substitute. Ye are accepted in the Beloved. The Lord shows, to the repenting, believing one, that Christ accepts the surrender of the soul, to be molded and fashioned after His own likeness."—*Selected Messages,* Book Two, pp. 32, 33.

We'd love to send you a free catalog of titles we publish
or even hear your thoughts, reactions, criticism,
about things you did or didn't like about this
or any other book we publish.

Just write or call us at:

TEACH Services, Inc.
254 Donovan Road
Brushton, New York 12916-9738
**1-800/367-1998**

http://www.TEACHServicesInc.com